Beyond the Ethical Demand

K. E. LØGSTRUP

Beyond the Ethical Demand

Introduction by Kees van Kooten Niekerk

University of Notre Dame Press
Notre Dame, Indiana

English language edition copyright © 2007 by University of Notre Dame
Notre Dame, Indiana 46556
www.undpress.nd.edu
All Rights Reserved

Designed by Wendy McMillen
Set in 11.3/13.4 Centaur MT and Eurostile by EM Studio
Printed on 60# Williamsburg Recycle paper in the U.S.A. by Versa Press, Inc.

English translations by Susan Dew and Heidi Flegal from K. E. Løgstrup's
Kunst og etik (1961), *Opgør med Kierkegaard* (1968), *Etiske begreber og problemer*
(1996 [1971]), *Norm og spontaneitet* (1972), and *System og symbol* (1982), published
by Gyldendal. Danish editions copyright © Gyldendal Publishing House,
Copenhagen.

Library of Congress Cataloging-in-Publication Data

Løgstrup, K. E. (Knud Ejler), 1905–
Beyond the ethical demand / K.E. Løgstrup, ; introduction by
Kees van Kooten Niekerk.
p.   cm.
Includes index.
ISBN-13: 978-0-268-03407-8 (pbk. : alk. paper)
ISBN-10: 0-268-03407-9 (pbk. : alk. paper)
1. Ethics. I. Title.
BJ78.D3L6213   2007
170—dc22

                              2007030325

Contents

Preface

The idea of publishing an English translation of central texts from K. E. Løgstrup's later ethical work arose at an international workshop organized by the Løgstrup Archive and held at the Sandbjerg Estate in Denmark from 8 to 12 May 2002. The workshop's subject was the significance of Løgstrup's ethics. Since most of Løgstrup's ethical publications after his major work *The Ethical Demand* were not available in English, three central extracts from those publications were translated into English. These translations were sent to the participants as preparatory material, and the speakers were asked to take account of them in their lectures. Thus they became an important part of the background for the contributions to the workshop, which are being published as *Concern for the Other: Perspectives on the Ethics of K. E. Løgstrup* simultaneously with the present volume.

At the workshop a decision was made to publish these extracts, along with a number of others, in order to give the English-speaking world the opportunity to become acquainted with the later Løgstrup's ethical thinking. This volume is the result. The original extracts ("The Sovereign Expressions of Life," "Sovereign Expressions of Life, the Golden Rule, Character Traits, and Norms," and "Expressions of Life and Ideas") have been translated by Susan Dew, who is a native English-speaker living in Denmark and has a degree in philosophy. The additional extracts ("Rejoinder," "Politics and Ethics," and "Norms and Expressions of Life") have been translated by Heidi Flegal, a bilingual professional translator also living in Denmark. The involvement of two translators with different backgrounds is inevitably reflected in a difference of style. However, in my function as editor, I have tried to ensure conformity in the key concepts and expressions used. Finally, George Pattison, now Lady Margaret Professor of Divinity at the University of Oxford, has been so kind as to subject the translations to a critical review, which has resulted in many improvements. This does not alter the fact, of course, that the ultimate responsibility for the translations lies with the translators and the editor, and reflects their choices in dealing with Løgstrup's characteristic prose style.

This book is the product of the cooperation of many people and several institutions. First and foremost I would like to thank the Velux Foundation for its generous funding of the Sandbjerg workshop and this translation. Second, I thank the two translators for the fine work they have done, Susan Dew especially for her unfailing willingness to discuss the subtleties of Løgstrup's expressions and improve the language, Heidi Flegal especially for her professionalism, flexibility, and humorous comments. Furthermore, great thanks are due to George Pattison for his generous and competent review of the translated text.

I am grateful to Alasdair MacIntyre for his support of the project and his intercession with the University of Notre Dame Press. I would also like to thank my colleague Svend Andersen for his general support and his aid in finding the right extracts. Moreover, I thank both him and David Bugge for many valuable comments on an earlier version of my introduction. Finally, I am grateful for the benevolent and stimulating cooperation I have had with Jeffrey Gainey, Chuck Van Hof, and Rebecca DeBoer at the University of Notre Dame Press, and for constructive comments from its reader.

Århus, Spring 2007
Kees van Kooten Niekerk

Introduction

Kees van Kooten Niekerk

Over the last fifteen years a new interest in the ethics of the Danish theologian and philosopher K. E. Løgstrup[1] has arisen in the Anglo-American world. This interest gave rise, among other things, to a new edition of his recognized book *The Ethical Demand* (University of Notre Dame Press, 1997; with an introduction by Hans Fink and Alasdair MacIntyre).

The Ethical Demand can be regarded as Løgstrup's principal ethical work. However, this by no means implies that *The Ethical Demand* gives a definitive account of the author's ethical thinking. Løgstrup continued to develop his ethical ideas long after 1956, when *Den etiske fordring*, the Danish original of *The Ethical Demand*, appeared, pursuing ethical topics until his death in 1981. And this development consisted not only in elaborations but also in substantial extensions and, in some respects, important modifications. Therefore, in spite of its central position in Løgstrup's ethical writings, *The Ethical Demand* conveys only a limited view of Løgstrup's ethical thinking as a whole. His ethics is much more complex and far richer than the ideas expressed there.

A part of this richness is contained in the six extracts from Løgstrup's later ethical writings presented here. Since these extracts have been taken from different books written during different periods of Løgstrup's thinking, a good understanding of them requires a certain acquaintance with the development of that thinking after *The Ethical Demand*. It is in order to meet this requirement that I shall not only present the principal ideas of these fragments, but also try to elucidate their relationship to *The Ethical Demand* and give some information about their background in Løgstrup's thinking as a whole.

1. Clarifications of *The Ethical Demand*

In the years after its appearance, *Den etiske fordring* gave rise to extensive discussion, both in Denmark and to a certain extent in the other Scandinavian countries. When Løgstrup published a collection of essays in 1961 entitled *Kunst og etik* (Art and Ethics), he took the opportunity to add a rejoinder to the main points of criticism leveled in that discussion. This Rejoinder contains a number of important elaborations on, and clarifications of, *The Ethical Demand*, which are helpful in gaining a better understanding of this book. To offer Anglo-American readers the same opportunity as Scandinavian readers, I have included Løgstrup's Rejoinder as chapter 1 here.

In this connection something should be said about Løgstrup's language. The Rejoinder is Løgstrup's reaction to a discussion that was sometimes conducted in a sharp polemical tone. Such a tone was not unusual in the theological circles to which Løgstrup belonged in the 1950s and 1960s. At some points in his Rejoinder, Løgstrup rebuts his critics using similar rhetorical means. This may be distressing for readers who are accustomed to a more courteous academic discourse. Løgstrup's polemical style should not deter them from reading on, however. For one thing, it reflects the author's existential concern for the matter, not a lack of seriousness. For another, and most importantly, Løgstrup's elaborations and clarifications are certainly worth one's while.

Let me mention just a few of them. In his introduction to *The Ethical Demand*, Løgstrup presents his conception of the ethical demand as an attempt to define "in strictly human terms" the relationship to other people that is contained in the proclamation of Jesus (Løgstrup 1997, 1). In other words, in *The Ethical Demand* Løgstrup claims to give a philosophical elucidation of the ethical demand, which is supposed to be accessible to all human beings, whether they are Christians or not. However, since this elucidation makes use of concepts that stem from the Christian tradition, it is not always clear whether Løgstrup is speaking as a philosopher or as a theologian. Especially when he states that the recognition of the one-sidedness of the ethical demand presupposes the understanding that life has been received as a gift (namely, from God), one might easily get the impression that Løgstrup is making a theological statement, thereby frustrating his elucidation of the ethical demand "in strictly human terms" (ibid., 116–118).

In his Rejoinder, Løgstrup removes this ambiguity. He makes a distinction between the Christian sphere and the human sphere. The former includes Jesus' granting of God's forgiveness and his issuing the ethical demand as God's demand. The latter includes the elucidation of the ethical demand in *The Ethical Demand*. This means, Løgstrup writes with reference to some of his critics, that "what I intended to say is that . . . 'the religious truth that life is a gift' and my 'religiously colored ontology,' or . . . . the questions of creation and of an absolute authority, do not belong within the realm of the particularly Christian, but within the realm of the human—they belong to a philosophical ethics." At the same time, however, he admits that in *The Ethical Demand*, he has not given a philosophical justification of the understanding that life is a gift from God. And he concedes that this flaw can only be defended with the "very trivial argument" that such a justification would be so demanding that it would have delayed the book by a decade!

As belonging to the human sphere, the ethical demand is specified at this point in the Rejoinder as "God's *universal* demand," which is "as old as creation." On the basis of this view Løgstrup maintains his rejection, put forward in *The Ethical Demand*, of a Christian ethics in the sense of an ethics that derives its norms from the Bible. In a discussion with the Danish theologian N. H. Søe,[2] who advocated such a Christian ethics, Løgstrup defends this rejection with the statement: "I regard it as a Christian claim that the ethical demand is not a specifically Christian demand." Obviously, Løgstrup endorses the idea of a *lex naturalis* given by God to his creation from the beginning. This idea was an element of his Lutheran tradition and constituted an important part of the theological background for his conception of the ethical demand. That is not to say that Løgstrup's ethics is nevertheless a Christian ethics, in the last resort, so to speak. Løgstrup's reference to *lex naturalis* is precisely a theological justification of the possibility of a strictly human or philosophical ethics. Consequently, Løgstrup also opposes the Swedish theologian Gustaf Wingren's[3] claim that the social norms can only be criticized adequately on the basis of the gospel. He maintains the view implicit in *The Ethical Demand* that such criticism can and should be exercised on the basis of the ethical demand. But he then goes on to add that a criticism of this kind would not differ from a criticism on the basis of the gospel. That is not to say that, for Løgstrup, Christian faith has no significance for social ethics. However, this significance does not consist in a specifically Christian criticism of the social norms, but rather in an extra incentive, drawn from belief in the Kingdom of God, to exercise a human or philosophical criticism.

Considering the fact that Løgstrup, in *The Ethical Demand*, offers a philosophical ethics, it is natural to ask on what kind of philosophy this ethics is based. In *The Ethical Demand* Løgstrup is not very specific on this point. We learn little more than that we must proceed "from the standpoint of our own existence" (Løgstrup 1997, 7), and that his analysis of trust is "of a phenomenological character" (ibid., 15). On this point the Rejoinder contains clarifying remarks, too: Løgstrup makes it clear that "[i]n my description of the phenomena, I have only worked with comparisons and distinctions within the natural language's interpretation of life. In short, I have stuck to phenomenological analyses and steered clear of scientific investigations."

The type of phenomenology referred to here goes back to the work of the German philosopher Hans Lipps, whose lectures Løgstrup attended in 1931–1932, and from whom he claimed to have learned the most.[4] Lipps's phenomenology shares with Heidegger's existential phenomenology the presupposition that human existence or *Dasein* involves a fundamental understanding of one's "being-in-the world." It is the task of phenomenology to interpret this understanding. However, Lipps's phenomenology differs from Heidegger's in two respects. First, whereas Heidegger is only interested in human "being-in-the-world" insofar as it reveals *Dasein*'s basic existential-ontological structure, Lipps analyzes many ways of "being-in-the world" for their own sake, in order to understand human existence in its concrete multiplicity. Second, unlike Heidegger, Lipps takes his point of departure in an analysis of the word usage in natural language, led by the conviction that such usage contains a fundamental understanding of human "being-in-the-world." It is this type of phenomenology that Løgstrup learned from Lipps and adopted as the methodological basis for his analyses of human conduct in *The Ethical Demand*. His description of the difference between anger and hate (Løgstrup 1997, 32–35, with references to Lipps) is a good example.

There is, however, an important difference between Løgstrup and Lipps (and Heidegger), in that Løgstrup used phenomenology not merely to describe human existence but also as a way to establish a normative ethics. Also on this point the Rejoinder is clarifying, because Løgstrup uses it to elucidate how he sees the relationship between phenomenology and ethics. In a reply to the objection that he has covertly implanted a positive evaluation in his analysis of trust, Løgstrup answers that positivity is not a quality *we* add to trust, but one that belongs to trust *itself*. Therefore a phenomenological analysis, though neutral in itself, describes trust as a positive phenomenon. And since phenomenology articulates a fundamental understanding given with human existence, the ultimate reason for the recognition of the ontological positivity of trust is this: "My life has given me to understand what is good and evil before I take a position on the issue and evaluate it."

Finally, these reflections give us a background for understanding Løgstrup's rejoinder to the criticism that in *The Ethical Demand* he committed the naturalistic fallacy. This criticism concerns Løgstrup's claim that the ethical demand arises out of the fact that people surrender themselves in trust to one another. With regard to this claim, many critics had objected that Løgstrup had not accounted sufficiently for the transition from fact to demand. Løgstrup replies that these critics erroneously supposed that he was speaking of a scientific fact. Had he meant a scientific fact, the transition would indeed have been a leap. But by "fact" he meant a fact as it appears to us as enterprising and emotional beings, before it has been subjected to scientific reduction. It is this kind of fact that is expressed in the natural language, which is the point of departure for Løgstrup's phenomenological analyses. And Løgstrup states that there is "the most intimate connection" between the fact of self-surrender in trust in this sense and the ethical demand. The reason is that as enterprising and emotional beings we cannot help but take a position on the other person's self-surrender in trust to us.

2. The sovereign expressions of life

In an article from 1967, the Danish theologian Ole Jensen[5] has drawn attention to a peculiar ambiguity in *The Ethical Demand*. According to Jensen, Løgstrup on the one hand connects the ethical demand with trust as a fact and speaks of "the realities of trust and love," which manifest the goodness of life (Løgstrup 1997, 141). On the other hand, however, he states that he operates with natural love as "an imaginary entity," because actually we know only "a natural love to which we have given our own self's selfish form." Similarly, there is no unadulterated trust, because we "hold ourselves in reserve instead of surrendering ourselves" (ibid., 138–139).[6] In the extract from *Opgør med Kierkegaard* (Controverting Kierkegaard) that has been included here ("The Sovereign Expressions of Life," chapter 2 in this volume), Løgstrup subscribes to Jensen's criticism and claims unambiguously that trust and natural love are realities in human life.

The reason is that in the meantime Løgstrup has developed the conception of what he calls "the sovereign expressions of life." The sovereign expressions of life are, roughly speaking, spontaneous other-regarding impulses or modes of conduct such as trust, mercy, and sincerity. Their characterization as "sovereign" is meant to indicate that they have the power to precede, or break through, our selfishness and express themselves in our behavior. Løgstrup gave his first detailed account of the sovereign expressions of life in 1968, in his book *Opgør med Kierkegaard* (Controverting Kierkegaard). Because this account is of seminal importance for the ethics of the later Løgstrup, it naturally found a place in the present volume.

It is not easy, however, to get a good grip of this account. The main reason is that it is embedded in a discussion with Kierkegaard in which Løgstrup controverts the latter's view of Christian belief. The understanding of some passages therefore presupposes a certain familiarity with Kierkegaard. Another reason is that Løgstrup takes his point of departure in an interpretation of Jean-Paul Sartre's play *Le diable et le bon dieu*, which he uses to illustrate some of Kierkegaard's ideas. Sartre's play, in turn, induces Løgstrup to consider Goethe's play *Goetz von Berlichingen*, which has the same protagonist in Goetz, an army commander at the time of the German peasant revolt during the Reformation. Løgstrup's references to these plays nicely exhibit a characteristic feature of his method, namely, combining phenomenological analyses with the interpretation of fiction. But they also complicate the reader's understanding, insofar as this becomes dependent on a certain acquaintance with the fiction. For these reasons, a few introductory remarks are in order. In the present context I restrict myself to Løgstrup's relationship to Kierkegaard. Information about the plays is given in a prefatory note to the text.

In 1950 Løgstrup gave a series of lectures at the Free University in Berlin in which he compared Kierkegaard's and Heidegger's analyses of human existence (published in Løgstrup 1950). According to Løgstrup, one of the main differences is that whereas Heidegger understands existence pre-ethically as *Sorge* (concern), Kierkegaard understands existence as basically defined by an infinite demand. In his evaluation of these thinkers Løgstrup subscribes to Kierkegaard's point of view. But at the same time he distances himself from Kierkegaard's *specification* of the infinite demand. According to Løgstrup, Kierkegaard construes the infinite demand on the basis of the absolute difference between God and humanity. As a consequence, its ultimate content is determined as the demand to express human inability and guilt face to face with God. Thus, in the last resort, Kierkegaard's infinite demand is a *religious* demand, not an ethical one. For Kierkegaard, moral life is only an occasion for the infinite demand, since it may make us aware of our inability and guilt. But by virtue of its religious nature, the infinite demand has no moral content. In contradistinction to Kierkegaard, Løgstrup defines the infinite demand as an *ethical* demand, which demands that we take care of the other for the other's sake. In his elaborations of this idea Løgstrup laid the ground for his conception of the ethical demand.

In the "Polemical Epilogue" of *The Ethical Demand,* Løgstrup turned his attention to Kierkegaard's *Works of Love,* which seemed to contradict his thesis that Kierkegaard only acknowledged a religious demand. In Løgstrup's view, however, there is no contradiction. He points out that for Kierkegaard love of the neighbor consists in helping one's neighbor to love

God. One reason is that this is best for one's neighbor; another is that only thus can love be self-denial. If the Christian were to serve the neighbor's welfare, the latter would applaud it, and that would spoil the former's self-denial. But this does not happen if the Christian helps the neighbor to love God. This love will be interpreted as hate by one's neighbor, and the Christian will be hated, despised, and persecuted for it by the world. Løgstrup concludes: "What is important to Kierkegaard is to be consistent in self-denial" (Løgstrup 1997, 222). This conclusion is in line with Løgstrup's earlier perception that what matters for Kierkegaard is the individual's self-renouncing relationship to God.

In the same context Løgstrup points out that Kierkegaard, in *Concluding Unscientific Postscript*, contrasts a religious relationship to God with living in immediacy, in which people have high ideas of their own abilities. Løgstrup rejects this way of opposing religion to immediacy. He blames Kierkegaard for not distinguishing between "immediacy" as devotion to one's work and fellow humans and "immediacy" in the selfish form we give it. The latter must, of course, be condemned, whereas the former must not, since it reflects our zest for life. And taken by itself (that is, apart from the selfish form we give it), zest for life is a positive thing (ibid., 234–235).

In *Opgør med Kierkegaard,* Løgstrup makes the Kierkegaardian contrast between religion and immediacy the central frame of reference for his exposition of the sovereign expressions of life. The reason is that the sovereign expressions of life as spontaneous phenomena belong to the sphere of immediacy. As such they constitute, for Løgstrup, a positive way of living, which is radically different from Kierkegaard's ideal of the individual's relationship to God. Because of this contrast Løgstrup stresses here the reflective (in the sense of self-reflective) aspects of Kierkegaard's ideal as a turn from immediate devotion to the world and one's neighbor to a reflective preoccupation with one's inner self. Needless to say, Løgstrup cannot accept that a true relationship to God should depend on such a turn. Instead he stresses that the fulfillment of the sovereign expressions of life already involves a true relationship to God.

This background illuminates some central aspects of Løgstrup's exposition of the sovereign expressions of life. For Kierkegaard, as Løgstrup interprets him, the individual can only become an authentic self through reflection as the way to a religious relationship to God. In opposition to this view, Løgstrup claims in "The Sovereign Expressions of Life" that the human person "no longer has to reflect about becoming his own person, nor has he to concern himself about becoming his true self; he has only to realize himself in the sovereign expression of life, and it is that expression of life—rather than reflection—that secures for a person his being himself." Løgstrup even connects this kind of being oneself with freedom. What Kierkegaard designated as humanity's fundamental "freedom of existence," in Løgstrup's opinion "consists in the sovereign expressions of life." Thus the sovereign expressions of life assume the function of conveying authentic existence, which Kierkegaard attributed to religious reflection. To be sure, Løgstrup merely criticizes Kierkegaard for thinking that "*only* through religious reflection can the human person accomplish the task of becoming a self" (emphasis added). In other words, he does not deny that we *may* become authentic persons through religious reflection. At the same time, however, it is obvious that Løgstrup regards being oneself in the sovereign expressions of life as the proper mode, or at least the preferred mode, of living authentically.

For Løgstrup the sovereign expressions of life also have a religious dimension. According to him they have been given to us by God to enable us to live our lives together. Thus the sovereign expressions of life are not only an alternative to Kierkegaard's idea of authenticity through religious reflection. They also constitute an alternative way of being related to God. Again, Løgstrup does not present this way as an exclusive alternative. He agrees with Kierkegaard that God also creates the self for eternity by placing the human being in what the latter calls "movements of infinity." But he does criticize Kierkegaard for his one-sidedness: "[W]hat he ignored was the fact that eternity creates the self not only for eternity but for the neighbor too, by investing him with the sovereign expressions of life as possibilities that match the claims in which eternity incarnates itself in the interpersonal situation." Here we meet an important aspect of the difference between Løgstrup's view of Christian belief and the view he ascribes to Kierkegaard. And it is natural to consider Løgstrup's religious understanding of the sovereign expressions of life as an elaboration of his thesis, already presented in the introduction of *The Ethical Demand,* that "it is in the relationship to our neighbor that the relationship to God is determined" (Løgstrup 1997, 4).

Løgstrup's critical attitude towards Kierkegaard's view of human relationship to God throws light on his inclusion of Sartre's *Le diable et le bon dieu*. In Løgstrup's interpretation, Sartre's Goetz exemplifies a person who lives in a movement of infinity, though in an inauthentic manner. First he does so by trying to be absolutely evil, later by trying to prove that it is possible to be absolutely good. He gives all he owns to the poor. But the poor do not benefit from it. According to Løgstrup, the reason is that Goetz is religiously preoccupied with himself, not with the fate of the poor. Good actions "confer benefits and happiness upon our neighbor only if they proceed on terms that are a-religious, purely human." Løgstrup draws a parallel to Kierkegaard's preoccupation with the absolute good in his interpretation of the commandment of love as helping the neighbor to love God. What Løgstrup wants to say is, I think, that the religious movement of infinity easily leads to aberrations, and at any rate does not benefit the neighbor, because the agent is fundamentally preoccupied with himself or herself.

In this extract from *Opgør med Kierkegaard*, Løgstrup also addresses the question of the relationship between the sovereign expressions of life and the ethical demand. In *The Ethical Demand* he had stated that human selfishness prevents the ethical demand from being fulfilled in the radical sense of acting exclusively for the sake of the neighbor. In the present extract he states that it is the sovereign expressions of life and their works that are demanded. Consequently, the demand is fulfilled in the realization of the sovereign expressions of life. But this fulfillment is a *spontaneous* one, not a fulfillment in conscious obedience to the demand. In the latter sense, the demand remains unfulfillable: "The demand is unfulfillable, the sovereign expression of life is not produced by the will's exerting itself to obey the demand." It is not until the sovereign expression of life fails that the demand makes itself felt—but at that point fulfillment is no longer possible. This leads Løgstrup to the conclusion that "the demand demands that it be itself superfluous." That is, by demanding something that can only be realized spontaneously, without being demanded, the demand in reality demands that it should not be necessary that it make itself felt as a conscious demand.

The ethical demand belongs within the sphere of morality, which Løgstrup distinguishes expressly from the "pre-moral" sovereign expressions of life. In his treatment of morality, Løgstrup once again stresses the role of (self-)reflection. In contradistinction to the ethics of custom, modern morality is characterized by reflection, not only on the content of morality but also on the question as to why one should be moral at all. This question involves a duplication in the sense that one reflects not only on what is morally right, but also on one's own relationship to that which is supposed to be morally right—which duplication is expressed in Hegel's question, "Have I a duty to duty?" Building on a positive answer, modern morality is acting out of duty, or out of virtue as a disposition to act out of duty. But, according to Løgstrup, such morality is a "delivery of substitute motives to substitute actions." It is so because it is a substitute for the pre-moral sovereign expressions of life in which a person's actions are motivated by a spontaneous preoccupation with the needs of the other, without reflecting on himself or herself as a moral person. And from Løgstrup's critical attitude to Kierkegaard's ideal of reflection as well as to conscious obedience to the ethical demand, it is clear that he regards acting out of the sovereign expressions of life as superior to moral action—although he acknowledges, of course, that the latter "is better than brutality or indifference."

3. Sovereign expressions of life, character traits, and norms

In his ethical works after *Opgør med Kierkegaard*, Løgstrup continued to be preoccupied with his conception of the sovereign expressions of life. This led him not only to elaborate this conception, but also to determine its relationship to other moral phenomena such as character traits and norms. The present volume includes two central extracts resulting from this preoccupation: "Sovereign Expressions of Life, the Golden Rule, Character Traits, and Norms" (chapter 3, hereafter SGCN), from the book *Norm og spontaneitet* (Norm and Spontaneity), which appeared in 1972; and "Norms and Expressions of Life" (chapter 4, hereafter NEL), from the collection of essays entitled *System og symbol* (System and Symbol), which appeared in 1982, one year after the author's death. As their titles suggest, these extracts to some extent deal with the same subjects. I will therefore provide them with a common introduction. Together they give a representative (though certainly far from complete) picture of the development of Løgstrup's fundamental ethics after *Opgør med Kierkegaard*.

I begin by giving some information about the books from which these extracts have been taken. *Norm og spontaneitet* is divided into three parts.

While the first part addresses issues in fundamental ethics, the second deals with specific ethical notions such as guilt, fate, and power. In the third part Løgstrup discusses concrete ethical problems, especially those relating to sexuality and politics. *System og symbol* is a posthumously published collection of essays that Løgstrup was preparing for publication prior to his death in 1981. It comprises reflections on ethical theory, contributions on social and political problems, and a number of literary analyses.

In *Norm og spontaneitet* Løgstrup adds an important feature to his description of the sovereign expressions of life from *Opgør med Kierkegaard.* The sovereign expressions of life defy being made a means to other goals than their own, which is the immediate service of the neighbor. As soon as they are instrumentalized in this sense, their spontaneity is broken, which destroys them, and indeed turns them into their opposite. If mercy, for example, is made to serve oneself or a third party, it is no longer mercy but unmercifulness. At the same time, according to Løgstrup, such instrumentalization will affect the radicalness of the sovereign expressions of life. As appears from *The Ethical Demand* (Løgstrup 1997, 44–46), by the radicalness of the ethical demand, Løgstrup means its demanding that we act exclusively for the sake of the other. Applied to the sovereign expressions of life, this means that their radicalness consists "not in any masterly feat but simply in the fact that the least ulterior motive is excluded" (SGCN). Since instrumentalization provides the realization of the sovereign expressions of life with ulterior motives, it destroys their radicalness. In this connection Løgstrup returns to the idea that the ethical demand does not make itself felt until the sovereign expression of life fails. But now he identifies the ethical demand with the Golden Rule in its biblical form: "Do unto others as you would have them do unto you." Løgstrup likes this formulation because it enjoins us to act on the basis of our imagination of what the other needs. In his view this is an expression of the radicalness of the ethical demand. As a consequence, the later Løgstrup often speaks of "the Golden Rule" instead of "the ethical demand."

In *System og symbol* Løgstrup designates the radicalness of the sovereign expressions of life as their unconditionality. Their "quality of unconditionality . . . consists in defying any ulterior motive" (NEL). But here he adds that this unconditionality implies that the sovereign expressions of life defy justification. The reason is that any attempt to justify them will make them contingent on a goal different from their own and thus instrumentalize them—which, as noted above, is precisely what they forbid. That the sovereign expressions of life cannot be justified means that they confront us with an ultimate authority. Løgstrup makes this point in the context of a criticism that he levels against the attempt to justify moral norms by deriving them from general principles. According to him, this attempt ends in a decisionism with regard to the acceptance of the general principles. "What is lacking is the confrontation with an ultimate authority" (NEL).

One might ask: What vindicates Løgstrup's conception of the sovereign expressions of life, not least the claim that they confront us with an ultimate authority? Generally, of course, this conception is based on his phenomenological approach. We have already seen (in the preceding discussion of the Rejoinder) that, according to Løgstrup, phenomenological analysis gives access to the positivity or negativity that is inherent in some phenomena, trust being one example. In *Norm og spontaneitet* he returns to this idea and elaborates it in the context of a discussion of British moral philosophy in the twentieth century. He values this philosophy's analyses of general ethical terms such as "good," "evil," "right," and "wrong," but regrets the fact that the British moral philosophers after G. E. Moore did not examine substantive "ethically descriptive phenomena" such as trust, veracity, and cowardice.[7] According to Løgstrup it is characteristic of these phenomena that they "cannot be described in abstraction from their goodness or badness" (SGCN). They are sovereign in the sense that they "have intimated to me what is good and bad before I consider the matter myself and evaluate it." And Løgstrup adds, giving his definition of the sovereign expressions of life an epistemic twist: "This is the reason for calling the positive expressions of life sovereign" (SGCN). Here the recognition of the positivity of the sovereign expressions of life is represented as something they make me understand rather than an insight I acquire of my own accord. And it seems to me that there is only a short step from this thesis of their epistemic sovereignty to the idea that the sovereign expressions of life confront us with an ultimate authority.

In the included extract from *Norm og spontaneitet* Løgstrup also discusses the relationship between the sovereign expressions of life and character traits. He had already occupied himself with character traits in the article "Ethik und Ontologie" (Ethics and Ontology, 1960), which was translated into English and added as an appendix to the new 1997 edition of *The Ethical Demand*. There his treatment of character traits is embedded in an account of the origins of morality in people's preoccupation with the tasks and common projects of life. In such preoccupation, "[t]he demands are completely incorporated into the concrete situation and are not divorced from it in special reflection about its morality" (Løgstrup 1997, 274). Løgstrup's point is that the rules of human work and community naturally arise from this preoccupation and need not be the subject of explicit reflection in order to guide our action. It should be noted that in this context Løgstrup uses the concept of morality in a wider sense than in *Opgør med Kierkegaard*, including what could be called "pre-reflective morality." And regarding his positive view of immediate action, it is hardly surprising that his treatment of pre-reflective morality is not encumbered with the negative connotations that reflective morality has in *Opgør med Kierkegaard*.

Løgstrup makes a similar point regarding the character traits that are required for the performance of the tasks and common projects of life: "The task, the job, the community and cooperation produce morality as well as the character that follows from it" (Løgstrup 1997, 274). Thus he claims that the character traits that correspond to pre-reflective morality arise naturally alongside it, without being made the object of conscious training. He illustrates this claim with Joseph Conrad's story (in *The Nigger of the Narcissus*) of the black man Jimmy's rescue by four sailors from drowning.

These ideas return in *Norm og spontaneitet*. In the meantime, however, Løgstrup has developed his conception of the sovereign expressions of life. Therefore he has to answer the question of how to relate these ideas, especially his view of character traits, to that conception. First, Løgstrup points to some phenomenological differences between the sovereign expressions of life and character traits: the former primarily concern personal relations, whereas the latter primarily concern work or tasks; the former defy being made a means to other goals than their own, whereas the latter can serve both good and bad goals; finally, the former cannot be produced by practice, whereas the latter can. Second, Løgstrup claims that sovereign expressions of life and character traits can converge in a concrete situation "without it being possible to say . . . which is which" (SGCN). He illustrates this with the same story he used in "Ethics and Ontology." The difference is that now not only character traits but also sovereign expressions are said to participate in the sailors' rescue action. Because we have to do with immediate, pre-reflective moral action, the previous contrast between the sovereign expressions of life and morality has vanished. And from a systematic point of view one might say that Løgstrup's description of pre-reflective morality constitutes a kind of intermediate between his conception of the ethical demand and his conception of the sovereign expressions of life.

In *The Ethical Demand* Løgstrup discusses at length the relationship between the ethical demand and what he calls the "social norms," which is a comprehensive designation for law, morality, and convention. His development of the conception of the sovereign expressions of life entailed a similar task, namely, consideration of the relationship between these and the social norms. In *Norm og spontaneitet* he sets about performing this task by considering Stephen Toulmin's view that a concrete moral position has to be justified with reference to a general principle that expresses an accepted social practice. Løgstrup criticizes this view as a kind of moralism, which replaces regard for the other with conformity to moral rules. As an alternative justification he proposes making explicit the moral experience of the concrete situation. To be sure, Løgstrup does not deny that reference to general principles or norms may play a part in ethical argumentation. But he stresses that norms and principles are subordinate to moral experience: "Before the relevant requirements on agency are requirements imposed by principles, they are requirements imposed by the specific and concrete situation, which latter enjoin us to act in ways answering to ethical predicates with descriptive content . . . including especially requirements prescribing communicative acts whose descriptions involve such predicates—a sovereign expression of life, the showing of trust, the offering of help, veracity, and the like" (SGCN).

In *System og symbol* Løgstrup gives a further determination of the relationship between norms and the sovereign expressions of life. He points out that we do not become aware of the sovereign expressions of life until a failure or conflict or crisis disrupts our immediate preoccupation with the needs of the other. This may become an occasion to formulate the sovereign expressions of life as norms. Important norms are, or ought to be, based on the sovereign expressions of life: "An ethical norm does not become fundamental because it is general or abstract, but because it is founded in a spontaneous expression of life" (NEL). Such a norm owes its "ought" to the unconditionality of the expression of life. That is not to say, Løgstrup emphasizes, that the unconditionality or the norm's "ought" dissolves the need to deliberate. There is no direct road from the sovereign expression of life or norm to concrete action. Sovereign expressions of life and norms have to be concretized with reference to the circumstances of the situation, and this concretization is our own responsibility. As a consequence, to justify our actions "[i]t is out of the question to invoke the expression of life, even though it may have undergirded the action" (NEL). Obviously this line of thought corresponds to the view, put forward in *The Ethical Demand*, that the ethical demand does not bypass a person's own judgment, and that one's action cannot be justified by pointing to the prompting of the ethical demand (Løgstrup 1997, 105–106).

Løgstrup's thesis that the sovereign expressions of life, by virtue of their unconditionality, confront us with an ultimate authority reminds us of another claim he put forward in *The Ethical Demand*: that the demand places "a person face to face with an ultimate authority which insists that the demand is fulfillable" (Løgstrup 1997, 171). This ultimate authority is God, the Creator (ibid., 167). Løgstrup's use of the same term in connection with the sovereign expressions of life suggests that "ultimate authority" has a religious connotation in this context as well. Actually, in the last section of the present extract from *System og symbol* Løgstrup explains why he thinks that the sovereign expressions of life point to a divine creator. One reason is the expression's sovereignty, which indicates that it does not stem from us. Another is its unconditionality. This unconditionality "bears witness to the fact that it [the sovereign expression of life] is not created by us, but comes from the universe" (NEL).

One might wonder why Løgstrup does not say that the sovereign expressions of life were created by a divine power, or by God, but merely says that they come from the universe. The reason is, I think, that he speaks as a philosopher here and, consequently, does not wish to go beyond what he regards as metaphysical speech. As was already noted in Fink and MacIntyre's introduction to the new edition of *The Ethical Demand*, during the last decade of his life Løgstrup drew together his philosophical views in a four-volume publication with the common title *Metafysik* (see Løgstrup 1997, xxvii–xxviii). This is not the place to give an account of Løgstrup's metaphysics. Even so, I draw attention to one aspect of this work that may explain his speaking of the universe in the present context. In the volume on the philosophy of religion, entitled *Skabelse og tilintetgørelse* (Creation and Annihilation),[8] Løgstrup makes a distinction between the transitions from experience to metaphysics and from metaphysics to religion. The former is asserted to have the character of an analytical judgment (in the Kantian sense of the word). Løgstrup illustrates this with the sovereign expressions of life: their unconditionality is a metaphysical feature that is entailed by the experience that they are destroyed by being made dependent on other goals than their own. On the other hand, the transition from metaphysics to religion is asserted to be synthetic, because it has the character of an imaginative interpretation that transcends empirical experience (cf. Løgstrup 1995a, 241–251).

By his pointing to the unconditionality of the sovereign expressions of life in our context, Løgstrup has moved into what he himself regards as a metaphysical discourse. In combination with the evolutionary view of human descent (to which Løgstrup subscribes in our text), this means that that unconditionality and the concomitant "ought" must come from the universe. This is still metaphysics in Løgstrup's sense of the word, because we have not left the empirical world. Had Løgstrup said that the sovereign expressions of life were created by God, he would have made the transition from metaphysics to religion. And that was not his purpose in a purely philosophical essay on an ethical subject. For his religious interpretation of the sovereign expressions of life we must turn to *Skabelse og tilintetgørelse* (Løgstrup 1995a, 89–92), to which Løgstrup himself refers at the end of our text (NEL).

4. Ethics and politics

The Ethical Demand is mainly concerned with individual ethics, that is, with the question of how individual persons should live their lives in relation to other persons. That is not to say that *The Ethical Demand* does not deal with social and political issues, but it does so primarily from the point of view of how the moral agent faced with the ethical demand should relate to the social and political world as a given reality. It does not contain normative reflections on how society ought to be arranged and ruled. However, this restriction should not be taken as characteristic of Løgstrup's ethics as a whole. Both before and after *The Ethical Demand*,

Løgstrup put forward many normative considerations about social and political questions, especially in *Norm og spontaneitet* and *System og symbol*. It is not possible to offer a representative selection of these considerations in a volume like the present one. Instead, we have chosen to present two extracts (chapters 5 and 6 in this volume) that deal with the relationship between ethics and politics in general—"politics" taken in the wider sense of reflection on social and political issues. More precisely, these extracts concern the relationship between the two key conceptions of Løgstrup's ethics—the ethical demand and the sovereign expressions of life—and politics. The purpose is to give the reader a first impression of the scope of Løgstrup's ethical thinking as a whole.

In *The Ethical Demand* the social and political world is addressed under the heading of social norms. The overarching question is how the individual who wants to comply with the ethical demand should relate to these norms. Løgstrup's answer is that, on the one hand, these norms have a guiding role for the specification of the ethical demand, because they have the function to protect us from exploitation by one another. On the other hand, however, their guidance is insufficient. For one thing, adherence to the motive of the demand, namely, concern for the other for the other's sake, is often decisive for an appropriate specification. For another, we should allow for the possibility that social norms become obsolete, in which case observing them may even cause violence (Løgstrup 1997, 53–63). This fairly positive view of the social norms does not mean that Løgstrup is not aware of their historical relativity. On the contrary, he discusses this relativity at length and illustrates it using a number of historical examples. However, according to Løgstrup their historical relativity does not detract from the guiding role of the social norms, because in a given historical situation they are highly determinative of the view of good and evil for those who have grown up in this situation, and thus for the concretization of the ethical demand (ibid., 64–104).

With reference to this view it is understandable that Wingren could accuse Løgstrup of uncritical acceptance of the existing social norms, and even compare his position to that of the German theologian Friedrich Gogarten (whose theological endorsement of the existing social norms in the 1930s functioned as a legitimation of Nazism).[9] But it was easy for Løgstrup, in his Rejoinder, to reject Wingren's accusation by pointing to his considerations about the insufficiency of the guidance provided by the social norms. In this connection he emphasizes the ethical demand's critical function with regard to the social norms.

This emphasis set the stage for Løgstrup's later attempts to determine the relationship between ethics and politics. Generally speaking, these attempts are characterized by seeking a viable route between two extremes: the view that politics can be deduced from ethics, on the one hand, and the view that there is no connection between ethics and politics, on the other.

This is already manifest in the first extract included here as chapter 5, the section "Politics and Ethics" from a lengthy essay entitled "Etiske begreber og problemer" (Ethical Concepts and Problems), which was published in 1971 as Løgstrup's contribution to a Scandinavian book on ethics and Christian belief.[10] Here Løgstrup contends that it is impossible to arrange society on the basis of the expectation that people will live by the ethical demand or, as he prefers to call it at this stage, the Golden Rule. Human egoism prevents this. One year later, in *Norm og spontaneitet*, Løgstrup would illustrate this point aptly with reference to the field of economics. The economic arrangement of society, he states, has to incorporate profit and competition, taking account of human egoism. Without it people work only on command, and only if they are monitored. If they are not, they merely work to meet their own basic needs. This was precisely what happened in the Soviet Union after World War I. As a result millions of people starved to death. Løgstrup concludes, laconically: "So dangerous is it to be moral" (Løgstrup 1972, 184; my translation). On the other hand, according to Løgstrup, it would be just as mistaken to banish ethics from politics. At the end of "Politics and Ethics" he attacks a proposal in this vein, as it was made by the German-Danish social scientist Theodor Geiger.[11] Geiger had argued that cooperation in a complex, large society cannot be based on feelings such as love and sympathy, but has to be ensured by an objective order in which there is no room for moral feelings. Løgstrup agrees with Geiger that we need an objective order, but denies that this should exclude ethics from politics: the objective order can, and should, be inspired by ethical considerations.

According to Løgstrup this can be done when we "moderate morality for use in our society." That is to say, the love commandment or the Golden Rule must be transformed into a political idea on the basis of which society should be ordered such that people are compelled to "act as though they loved their neighbor, knowing full well that they do not." Løg-strup shows the implications of this transformation by imagining how the Good Samaritan would behave if, in an attempt to put an end to rob-bery between Jerusalem and Jericho, he decided to become a "Political Samaritan."

The other extract, included here as chapter 6, is the essay "Expres-sions of Life and Ideas" taken from *System og symbol*. This extract deals with the relationship between the sovereign expressions of life and po-litics. It is Løgstrup's central claim that the sovereign expressions of life constitute the foundation upon which our rationality builds. But they themselves cannot be rationalized, that is, incorporated into the rational structure of society. At the same time, however, without the sovereign ex-pressions of life this structure would collapse, since, as Løgstrup puts it, they are responsible for "sustaining the whole." Obviously he is thinking of the fact, mentioned above, that without the sovereign expressions of life, communal life would cease to exist. Were it not for natural trust, open-ness of speech, and mercy, human communication and cooperation would not be possible. As a consequence, our rationally structured life together would not be able to function, because it builds on communication and cooperation.[12]

As the title of this extract suggests, Løgstrup is dealing here with the relationship between the sovereign expressions of life and the ideas or ide-als that underlie our organization of society. By analogy with his consid-erations in "Politics and Ethics," Løgstrup stresses that we cannot ground the social order in the sovereign expressions of life—first because they cannot be rationalized, and second because if we tried, we would fall victim to the illusion "that society could be founded on a high-minded morality." The ideas with which we organize society can have different sources, for example the need to tackle difficulties engendered by the ex-isting order. But whatever their sources, it is the function of the sovereign expression of life to be a touchstone in the question of "whether our ideas banish the expressions of life from the social order."

Løgstrup exemplifies his argument with the idea of equality. In mo-dernity this idea has come to be of central importance for the foundation of the social order. It has a positive function as a safeguard against the ar-bitrary distribution and exercise of power. But if it is construed as the idea of an equal opportunity that gives way to ruthless competition, it is converted from a life-affirming principle into a life-denying one. Indeed it is precisely mercy, the sovereign expression of life, that, used as a touchstone, makes us realize this.

Løgstrup's preoccupation with the idea of equality moves him to connect his reflections on the relationship between ethics and politics with his metaphysics in a way that reminds us of the way he connected his view of the sovereign expressions of life with his metaphysics at the end of the other extract from *System og symbol,* discussed above. According to Løgstrup in "Expressions of Life and Ideas," the political idea of equality is founded in an underlying equality "in which, by the hand of nature, we already find ourselves." Løgstrup has in mind what is usually called "human dignity," which is a kind of equality in the sense that it pertains equally to every human being, regardless of his or her contribution to the common good. He characterizes this equality in ways similar to the sovereign expressions of life: it "sustains the whole," political equality cannot be deduced from it, and it has to be a touchstone for the social order.

Løgstrup calls this equality "cosmic equality." The main reason he gives for this terminology is that as an attribute of human beings, this equality must have emerged from the universe through biological evolution. This raises the question as to how an apparently purely natural process can give rise to something so unconditional as cosmic equality. Løgstrup does not propose an answer here. But in *Ophav og omgivelse* (Source and Surroundings), one of his four volumes on metaphysics, he states that the unconditional nature of cosmic equality suggests a religious interpretation, which claims that a divine power is involved in the processes of the universe (Løgstrup 1995b, 104–106). It is easy to see that this argument is analogous to Løgstrup's above-mentioned metaphysical reflections about the unconditionality of the sovereign expressions of life and his pointing to their religious interpretation in *Skabelse og tilintetgørelse.*

Whatever one may think of the ideas described here, it can hardly be denied that they contain original, and sometimes eye-opening, views. Some of them may invite contradiction. But even the most critical reader can learn something from the extracts presented here. I consider some points particularly instructive: Løgstrup's acute phenomenological-psychological descriptions of what is going on in and between human beings; his taking such descriptions as the point of departure for ethical considerations, which gives his ethics a concrete character that is absent in much traditional ethics; his stress on our fundamental and beneficial dependence on the sovereign expressions of life, in opposition to the usual emphasis on human independence and autonomy; his nuanced and realistic attempts to relate ethics and politics; and finally—for those interested in theology— his connection between the sovereign expressions of life and the doctrine of creation. In my opinion these points convey as many reasons why, like *The Ethical Demand*, this volume deserves to find attentive readers.

Notes

1. For a survey of Løgstrup's life and work, the reader is referred to Hans Fink and Alasdair MacIntyre's introduction to the new edition of *The Ethical Demand* (Løgstrup 1997, xv–xxxviii).

2. Niels Hansen Søe (1895–1978) was Professor of Ethics and the Philosophy of Religion in Copenhagen from 1939 to 1965. His theological thinking was influenced decisively by Karl Barth. He is best known for his *Kristelig Etik* (Christian Ethics) from 1942, which appeared in five editions. Here, using the New Testament as his point of departure, he developed a specific Christian ethics based on God's revelation in Christ.

3. Gustaf Wingren (1910–2000) was Professor of Systematic Theology in Lund from 1951 to 1977. The overarching interest of his theological work was to relate a Lutheran view of Christian belief to human life, regarded in the perspective of the doctrine of creation. He drew inspiration from Løgstrup, among others. His interest is reflected in the titles of the two books in which he set out his understanding of Christian belief: *Skapelse och lagen* (1958; English edition: *Creation and Law*, 1961) and *Evangeliet och kyrkan* (1960; English edition: *Gospel and Church*, 1964).

4. Cf. the introduction to the new edition of *The Ethical Demand* by Fink and MacIntyre, Løgstrup 1997, xvi–xix. Although in his Rejoinder Løgstrup does not refer to Lipps, the many references to him in *The Ethical Demand* testify to his influence.

5. Ole Jensen (b. 1937) is a disciple of Løgstrup's. From 1974 to 1978 he was Professor of Systematic Theology in Copenhagen. In 1976 he obtained his doctoral degree in theology with the thesis *Theologie zwischen Illusion und Restriktion* (Theology between Illusion and Restriction), 1975, in which, on the basis of some of Løgstrup's ideas, he criticized German existentialist theology for supporting western environmental destruction. He is best known for his commitment to ecology and for his interpretations of Løgstrup's work.

6. Cf. Jensen 1994, 23–24.

7. Unfortunately, Løgstrup was apparently unfamiliar with British descriptivism as represented by, for example, Philippa Foot. At any rate he does not relate his considerations in *Norm og spontaneitet* about ethically descriptive phenomena to British descriptivism. For a general discussion of Løgstrup's treatment of British moral philosophy in the twentieth century, see Brenda Almond's contribution to Andersen and Niekerk (2007).

8. A two-volume translation into English of parts of Løgstrup's metaphysics was published in 1995 under the title *Metaphysics* by Marquette University Press. This translation includes the complete text of *Skabelse og tilintetgørelse* (Løgstrup 1995a) and a selection from the other three volumes (Løgstrup 1995b).

9. Friedrich Gogarten (1887–1967) was Professor of Theology in Breslau and Göttingen from 1931 to 1955. He was one of the initiators of the so-called dialectical theology in Germany in the 1920s. His principal theological interest was to connect Christian faith with responsible living in the world. In his *Politische Ethik* (1932), to which Wingren refers, he pleaded for conformity with the existing social order and glorified the state as the maintainer of that order. These ideas are put into relief by the fact that in 1933 he declared his support (though only temporarily) to the political group Die Deutsche Christen (The German Christians), who backed Nazism.

10. Løgstrup's essay was republished in 1996 as a book with the same title.

11. Theodor Geiger (1891–1952) emigrated in 1933 from Germany to Denmark. From 1938 to 1952 he was Professor of Sociology in Aarhus, with an interruption in 1940–1945 because of the war. He has concerned himself with many branches of sociology and is regarded as one of the founders of the concept of social stratification. His many publications include *Sociologi: Grundrids og hovedproblemer* (Sociology: Outline and Main Problems), 1939, which was the first Danish textbook of sociology since the nineteenth century, and *Die Gesellschaft zwischen Pathos und Nüchternheit* (Society between Pathos and Sobriety), 1960, to which Løgstrup refers.

12. Giddens 1991, chapter 3, can be seen as an explication of the role of trust for life in a rationalized society. See especially the author's emphasis on the importance of people's trust in the representatives of expert systems if they are to have confidence in the functioning of those systems (pp. 83–88).

References

Andersen, Svend, and Kees van Kooten Niekerk, eds. 2007. *Concern for the Other: Perspectives on the Ethics of K. E. Løgstrup*. Notre Dame: University of Notre Dame Press.

Giddens, Anthony. 1991. *The Consequences of Modernity*. Cambridge: Polity Press.

Jensen, Ole. 1994. *Sårbar usårlighed* (Vulnerable Invulnerability). Copenhagen: Gyldendal.

Løgstrup, K. E. 1950. *Kierkegaards und Heideggers Existenzanalyse und ihr Verhältnis zur Verkündigung* (Kierkegaard's and Heidegger's Analysis of Existence and Its Relationship to the Proclamation). Berlin: Erich Blaschker Verlag.

———. 1956. *Den etiske fordring* (The Ethical Demand). Copenhagen: Gyldendal.

———. 1961. *Kunst og etik* (Art and Ethics). Copenhagen: Gyldendal.

———. 1968. *Opgør med Kierkegaard* (Controverting Kierkegaard). Copenhagen: Gyldendal.

———. 1971. "Etiske begreber og problemer" (Ethical Concepts and Problems). In Gustaf Wingren, ed., *Etik och kristen tro*, 205–286. Copenhagen: Gyldendal.

———. 1972. *Norm og spontaneitet* (Norm and Spontaneity). Copenhagen: Gyldendal.

———. 1978. *Skabelse og tilintetgørelse* (Creation and Annihilation). Vol. 4 of *Metafysik*. Copenhagen: Gyldendal.

———. 1982. *System og symbol* (System and Symbol). Copenhagen: Gyldendal.

———. 1983. *Ophav og omgivelse* (Source and Surroundings). Vol. 3 of *Metafysik*. Copenhagen: Gyldendal.

———. 1995a and 1995b. *Metaphysics*. 2 vols. Milwaukee: Marquette University Press.

———. 1996. *Etiske begreber og problemer* (Ethical Concepts and Problems). Copenhagen: Gyldendal.

Løgstrup, Knud Ejler. 1997. *The Ethical Demand*. Notre Dame: University of Notre Dame Press.

Beyond the Ethical Demand

Rejoinder

The aim of the following pages is to consider some of the criticism that has been leveled against *The Ethical Demand* (1956). In doing so, I have chosen to disregard the shorter reviews, for although several of them offer interesting criticisms, they are not really written in such a way as to invite dialogue, their aim being merely to characterize and appraise the book in general terms for the reader. I therefore consider only the contributions that actually sought discussion.

Having to deal with hostile criticism does not in itself harm such a discussion. The issue is not whether there is agreement, but whether the points made are of a kind that serve to focus on the assumptions underlying the claims and the objections made to them. By the same token a discussion is not likely to be very stimulating if, as so often happens, the participants simply restate their initial positions, to the effect of "I never said x" or "I already said y." I have therefore disregarded objections that could only lead to this sort of discussion, and they have, in fact, been few and far between. Naturally, I have also faced objections to which I cannot reply, because I simply do not know how to respond.

I have had to choose between dealing with each critic separately, and arranging their objections and my responses systematically. The former

1

would, of course, be the most satisfactory solution for the critics, but it would be unbearable for the reader. The latter, while admittedly unsatisfactory from the critics' point of view, is the only acceptable solution for the reader. This is therefore the solution I have chosen.

1. Trust—distrust. Methodological divergences

I shall first deal with a contribution (printed in *Perspektiv* 1960, no. 8) bearing the innocuous title "A Response in the Discussion of the Ethical Demand," which, upon closer inspection, proved to be a most vehement attack on my position. In this contribution Henrik Stangerup begins by challenging my claim that we human beings normally meet one another with trust, and that special circumstances must be present before we show someone distrust. He contends that the opposite is rather the case: distrust comes first, or at least the first thing we show is a cautious, sceptical neutrality that tests the other person to sound out his strengths and weaknesses. Trust, on the other hand, follows after as "a result of the fulfillment of love or friendship."

To this I would say that the disagreement between Stangerup and myself is not merely, as he presumes, a question of what comes first and what comes last, trust or distrust. He and I take the words "first" and "last" to mean different things. The difference can be pinned down as follows: Stangerup is inquiring into which of the two comes first in time, and which comes last, whereas I see the difference between first and last more as a difference in rank, having my sights set on the foundational relation. When Stangerup says that distrust comes first, he means—and this is also how he expresses himself—that in a person's historically progressing existence, trust "follows after" distrust. When I, on the other hand, say that trust is primary, I mean that distrust is the negation of trust, and is, as such, founded in trust.

In other words, at the root of our mutual disagreement as formulated by Stangerup lies a difference in approach. Stangerup's objection gives me a welcome opportunity to elaborate on the methodological problem, which is this: Can one make a pronouncement about the foundational relation between two attitudes such as those we are dealing with here? In other words: Does a philosophical psychology exist alongside scientific psychology? I believe it does. But how should one proceed in order to clarify a foundational relation? I do not intend to offer a method for this, but only to mention three different paths by which I myself have moved forward.

1) I have taken the different roles that trust and distrust play for the child and the adult as indicators that trust is the fundamental attitude. The profound repercussions resulting from the abuse of a child's trust show how elemental an attitude trust is in the child. Likewise, a devaluation of trust—a reservation on the part of the adult, which is created by experience and conditioning, and which adults involuntarily use to prevent a breach of trust having the same fatal consequences for them as it does for a child—bears witness to distrust being secondary, and deriving from a negation of trust.

As far as this point is concerned, I regard the temporal relation as an indication of the foundational relation: The child is utterly involved in the trust and in the self-surrender it entails. The reason why I believe trust ranks above distrust is that initially (meaning in the child) trust is fully and completely unreserved, distrust arriving only with age, with the warnings that had to be issued, with the negative experiences that befall a person through his or her trust. The point is, the difference between child and adult lies not only in a person being a child first, and then becoming an adult; we all find that the two are essentially different kinds of existence. And do we not, indeed, regard the child's life as being, in certain respects, more true, more genuine than the adult's life—precisely because, among other things, trust plays such an enormous, decisive role?

Apart from this, Stangerup is forced to limit his own claim (that of distrust coming before trust) by conceding that it does not apply to the relationship between child and adult. From my point of view, however, this is not a coincidental limitation. This is exactly where the ranking between trust and distrust becomes evident. Stangerup also mentions in this connection that countless poets have told us in their works what a tragedy it is to grow up, since it is accompanied by the heart-breaking death of trust. From this Stangerup draws the conclusion that trust is not something fundamental to human life. I would say the approach one adopts depends on what one understands by "fundamental." The experiences of the poets show (and Stangerup is right in this observation) that distrust takes up at least as much space in our lives as does trust, and perhaps even a good deal more. But if one looks into the ranking of the concepts, the poets' experiences also show that distrust is founded in trust, as its negation.

2) In order to establish the foundational relation between trust and distrust, I have mentioned that one normally does not ask anyone to account for the trust they might have in someone else, but rather for their distrust of someone else. This cannot be explained from Stangerup's viewpoint, which would lead one to anticipate the opposite. Were it true that distrust temporally occurred first, so that we began with that, there would be no reason to ask someone to account for it. And similarly, if trust occurred next, following after as "a result of the fulfillment of love or friendship," a person's trust ought to be something they would normally be expected to account for. They would be expected to justify their trust through their experience of the other person's love and friendship. Yet as mentioned, the opposite is the case. We ask no one to account for their trust, which can only be explained by our establishing a foundational point of view that assumes trust to be the fundamental attitude.

3) Finally, I have proceeded in a way that seeks to show trust to be such an elemental phenomenon that it is also active in places where we fail to recognize it at all, for instance in the note we strike in a conversation with other people.

Whether Stangerup and I still disagree depends on the position he takes on the distinction I have made here, and which one could, perhaps, call a distinction between a psychological status report and an investigation of the foundational relation. For if I am correct in perceiving Stangerup's reflections on trust and distrust as such a status report, then I can follow his reasoning. The question is whether Stangerup, on his part, will concede that it is possible to practice a philosophical psychology that includes an explanation of the foundational relations, and whether he can follow my particular reasoning in favor of the foundational relation that I believe exists between trust and distrust. I can pose the same question to Professor Søe, who also criticizes my claim regarding the relationship between trust and distrust (in *Dansk teologisk Tidsskrift* [Danish Theological Journal], 1958, no. 1), although he does so less extensively than Stangerup and more in passing.

In this connection I must bring up another point, namely, Stangerup's claim that I confuse immediacy and trust. In Stangerup's view, what takes up space in our lives is immediacy, which is superficial. Trust, on the other hand, is a serious matter, and something we only place in a person we are sure of in advance.

My reply is that Stangerup's concept of trust and my concept are different. Stangerup sees trust as a complex phenomenon incorporating an experience of the other person's character and personality, which one has come to trust. I see trust as such an elemental phenomenon in our existence that, as mentioned earlier, I can also find it in the note we strike in a conversation. It is clear, however, that in seeing trust as an elemental phenomenon, I believe it is found in many more places than Stangerup's complex phenomenon. Trust as an elemental phenomenon is something we involuntarily show, and something that also belongs in our immediate life, but, be it noted, as an element in it. Stangerup can therefore say he prefers to regard trust as a complex phenomenon that does not belong to immediacy. But he cannot claim that I have confused trust and immediacy, as though I had not defined trust in such a way as to make it clear that trust is only one single, specific element occurring within the immediacy that is also hundreds of other things. One really cannot speak as summarily, as massively, about immediacy as Stangerup does. This makes one reason as though trust as a complex phenomenon opposed to immediacy were some kind of universal classification, so that the mere act of regarding trust as an elemental rather than a complex phenomenon meant identifying it with immediacy. But that is certainly no way to argue a point, and thus I have to reject Stangerup's accusation that I confuse trust with immediacy.

Another objection, but one that also addresses my methodology, has been presented by Gunnar Hillerdal in his work *Teologisk og filosofisk etik* (Theological and Philosophical Ethics) (Stockholm, 1958). He claims that from the outset I have covertly implanted an evaluation into my basic analysis of the relationship of trust. I deny that it is a question of such an implantation.

The point is this: trust and distrust are two ways in which human beings can understand their own lives and themselves, and what Hillerdal ignores in his reasoning is that one aspect of the self-understanding of trust is its positive character, just as the self-understanding of distrust includes its negative character. It is not an evaluation that is added on, and to which trust and distrust are subject; it belongs to the phenomena themselves. Therefore it is also embedded in the meaning of the two words. Evaluating trust as something negative goes against the very nature of trust itself, and goes against the meaning of the word. We are therefore barred from actually *understanding* trust as something negative. Another matter is that we can evaluate trust as something negative. However, we can only do so if we consider trust from a point of view that goes beyond what trust itself tells us—namely, that it is something positive. This is not just a theoretical possibility. It does sometimes happen that we evaluate trust negatively, despite its nature, because trusting is a dangerous thing in a given situation. Trust can be abused, and when raising our children we are therefore obliged to warn them against showing trust in certain circumstances. Yet this does not make trust a neutral phenomenon that we are free to understand either positively or negatively. We can only evaluate trust negatively in defiance of its self-understanding. It goes without saying that the same principle applies to a positive evaluation of distrust, which is only possible if we go against distrust's understanding of itself as something negative.

Whether something is positive or negative, good or evil, is not decided at the moment when we evaluate it; it is not originally decided at the moment when we make it our own. My life made me its own before I made it mine. My life has given me to understand what is good and evil before I take a position on the issue and evaluate it. Subsequently, as I have already mentioned, I can admittedly take the position that, in a given set of circumstances, the right thing is to promote that which life itself has taught me to regard as something negative. An example of this would be teaching a child to show distrust. In other words, our evaluation can go against the phenomena's self-definitions as good and evil, but it cannot invalidate these definitions. It cannot render the phenomena themselves ethically indifferent.

An ethics that is not to consist of a simplification must have room for both definitions—life's own definition of what is good and evil, which life has passed on to me, and the definition of what is good and evil that I choose when I take a position. But it is certainly strange that neither anti-metaphysical philosophy nor existentialism are prepared to recognize our life's own understanding of what is good and evil, and only recognize the definition we convey through our evaluation. It is striking to observe this similarity between antimetaphysical philosophy and existentialism, amidst all their manifest disparity.

Hillerdal is guilty of the same simplification and fails to consider the complicated nature of the matter. In objecting that from the beginning I "covertly implant an evaluation into [my] basic analysis of the relationship of trust," that I "move directly from an analysis of a generally occurring relationship, the relationship of trust, to the positive evaluation of it as something good," Hillerdal is presuming that not until we evaluate trust does it become a positive thing, and distrust a negative thing. But as noted earlier, that is not so: trust is something positive before our evaluation, and distrust something negative before our evaluation, which is why the phenomenological analysis can establish this. Indeed, it cannot help doing so. Hillerdal continues: "For a purely phenomenological analysis never, ever, leads to the conclusion that what it establishes is right and desirable." This objection, too, I must reject. Granted, the phenomenological analysis is, in and of itself, neutral, but the phenomenon it is investigating is not. If trust is the object of the analysis, its desirability is one of the qualities we become conscious of through the phenomenological analysis. On the other hand, Hillerdal is correct in declaring that an actual evaluation—be it in line with trust's own positivity or against it—has nothing to do with the phenomenological analysis. But it is not that definition of what is good and evil I have in mind. On the contrary, it is the definition of trust as good and distrust as evil, which I derive from trust and distrust themselves.

As I have already mentioned, Hillerdal shares the limitations of the views of antimetaphysical philosophers and existentialists, who state that the definitions "good" and "evil" do not arise until we make our evaluation. Here I would like to observe, however, that the correlate of the evaluation is a scientific investigation of phenomena that are neutral as far as positivity and negativity are concerned. For phenomena do not become neutral until subject to scientific investigation, which begins with an act of reduction—and among the things eliminated are positivity and negativity. If we are only dealing with phenomena that the scientific approach has divested of their ethical qualities, then clearly it is only through the efforts of an evaluation that they can once again be made ethical. Yes, Hillerdal does speak of "phenomenological analysis," but what he means is "scientific investigation." And he makes no distinction between the two. There is a distinction, however, and a decisive one at that: an analysis is termed phenomenological precisely because, unlike a scientific investigation, it does not seek to reduce the phenomenon.

2. Demand and fact

The vast majority of critics have objected that I have not fully accounted for the transition from fact to demand. I state that the lives of human beings are entwined with one another, and I then go on to say, with no further explanation, that this is the source from which the demand arises—the demand that we take care of the part of the other person's life that has been placed at our mercy. But a judgement about what *is* can never give rise to a judgement about what *ought to be*.

That objection, however, contains two issues that are intermixed, but which must be kept apart. 1) We must accept that we cannot merely describe and theorize, leaving it at that. We cannot exist without taking a position and intervening. We are, first and last, enterprising and emotional beings who therefore live through goals, actions, and decisions. It is therefore impossible in a given situation to recognize that the other person's life has been surrendered to one without taking a position in respect of that circumstance. Between fact and demand there is the most intimate connection. The demand arises directly out of the fact. Whether we wish to or not, we heed or disregard the demand of taking care of the other person's life, simply because both he and I live through enterprise and emotion, and not just through cognition. Therefore there is no problem in finding out how a demand arises out of a fact. It happens of its own accord and is, simply, unavoidable.

2) Another issue that has turned out to be a problem is that of determining whether one can say a demand is true. A cognitive act is true if it corresponds to the fact it claims to recognize—whatever one might understand by "corresponding to." But one cannot say a demand is true in that sense.

The difficulty in keeping the two problems separate is rooted in one's spontaneous understanding of "facts" as scientifically reduced data. It is quite right to say that there is a leap from such data to the demand, because we are then dealing with a transition from description and theory to the world in which we live enterprisingly and emotionally. This is how the objection understands the word "fact." I, on the other hand, understand something different by "facts," namely, the facts before they have been reduced by the sciences. Out of such facts, the demand arises directly. In my view, the discovery that so many have raised objections regarding my clarification of the relationship between demand and fact merely testifies to how much we are hectored by the view that the sciences have a monopoly on making pronouncements about reality. It also testifies to how urgent the need is for firmly establishing the difference between, on the one hand, a concrete life situation with its wealth of perspectives that intermingle without disturbing each other, and, on the other hand, the cross-sectional view of reality presented by the sciences; a view that comes about by virtue of what could be called "a scientific reduction."

Mogens Lund's objection (in an article in the Danish newspaper *Information*) is typical: I am, he asserts, welcome to say that one person's life is entwined with another's, since that is a neutral fact, whereas I may not say that one person holds another's life in their hands since, in so doing, I say more than is scientifically warranted. Lund involuntarily assumes that I am arguing scientifically to substantiate the fact out of which the demand arises.

However, from its first to its last page, *The Ethical Demand* contains not one single scientific sentence. If I were compelled to characterize my book methodologically, I would have to say that it is philosophical. It would, I might add, be meaningless to say it is theological, since "theology" does not denote a method, because we use various methods within the different theological disciplines.

If anyone objects that despite this, in my book I establish one fact after the other, then I have to say that the sciences are really not the only instruments for establishing facts. We also do this through our everyday language. And there are facts that everyday language is better at establishing than the sciences are. There are phenomena we can only describe and distinctions we can only express using natural language. That is why much philosophy remains within the interpretation of the world, of things, and of human existence that is given in our everyday language. Conversely, everyday language's "sorting" of things is useless in attempts to track down the laws in which the exact sciences are interested. In order to track these down, we must carry out a new and different classification of things, and that is what takes place in the so-called scientific languages. But as I said earlier, I have not sought to establish scientific laws. This I leave to psychology, sociology, and similar sciences. In my description of the phenomena, I have only worked with comparisons and distinctions within the natural language's interpretation of life. In short, I have stuck to phenomenological analyses and steered clear of scientific investigations.

3. Human—Christian

And now to the question of the human and Christian spheres.[1] I shall begin by setting out the difference as I see it. That which is unforeseen in the proclamation of Jesus—that is, the granting of God's forgiveness without regard for the qualifications of the person to whom it is granted—is that which is particularly Christian. It is also particularly Christian that a human being—Jesus of Nazareth—does not speak of the radical ethical demand in some philosophical reflection, but does what no human being has the right to do: he issues it as his own, and God's, demand, simply and directly, to another person or the people around him.

By contrast, the acknowledgment of the fact that the ethical demand is radical and one-sided in an understanding, experience, or interpretation of, or a belief in (or whatever else one might choose to call it), our life as something given to us belongs to the human sphere. If one calls it "belief," it is not a particularly Christian belief but a human one. If one calls it "religiousness," it is not a particularly Christian religiousness but a human one.

One characteristic of *The Ethical Demand* that makes it obvious that this is the way I distinguish between the human and the Christian spheres is the book's structure. First I analyse how the life of one person is interwoven with the life of another, and from this I deduce the content of the demand, which has to do with taking care of the life of the other person that has been surrendered to us. Some way into the book I make it clear that the one-sidedness of the demand cannot be deduced in this way, but presupposes that life has been given to the individual person. I have not thereby moved over to the particularly Christian sphere, however, but continue to clarify what can be stated in strictly human terms. My making this distinction is also evident in the penultimate chapter's explanation of the particularly Christian sphere, and in the fact that I do not deal with it before this point.

Having said this, I willingly concede that the language I use in the introductory chapter, in which I distinguish between "human" and "religious," is unfortunate and misleading. I should have distinguished between "human" and "Christian." At all events, what I intended to say is that (as Stangerup would express it) "the religious truth that life is a gift" and my "religiously colored ontology," or (to use Hillerdal's words) the questions of creation and of an absolute authority, do not belong within the realm of the particularly Christian, but within the realm of the human—they belong to a philosophical ethics.

But I also concede something else: whereas the interweaving of one person's existence with another person's, which gives the demand its content, is demonstrated through a number of phenomenological analyses, the understanding that life is given to the individual person, which is what makes the demand radical, is only presented as a claim, pure and simple. And I do indeed realize that when this claim is merely repeated without being treated phenomenologically, it seems neither convincing nor thought-provoking. On the contrary, it might even seem embarrassing. Stangerup says so—in his rather harsh manner—referring to the claim as "incredibly trite" and "clergyman's talk in its most diluted form." (I hope that someday Stangerup becomes a priest: I should like to hear him deliver a sermon.) If Stangerup means by this that the claim does not belong anywhere, then he and I disagree. If, on the other hand, he is taking issue with its poor form, I admit that he is pointing out a flaw. In defending myself I can only present a very trivial argument, which is this: were the understanding of life presumed by the radicality of the demand to have been as phenomenologically well elaborated as the fact from which the demand gains its content, another decade would have passed before I could have published my book. The reason is that the phenomenological analyses required to do so are of an altogether different nature.

Hillerdal finds it reasonable to interpret my presentation as if I had intended to give a philosophically sound analysis, to present a philosophical ethics and claim that in principle, it is a universal ethics (*Teologisk og filosofisk etik,* 170). Hillerdal is quite right in this observation: it is no misinterpretation.

What, then, does Hillerdal hold against my account? He has two main objections: first, that my philosophy is not antimetaphysical, and second, that my philosophical analysis corresponds all too well, indeed suspiciously well, with Christianity's view of moral life. I shall deal with these two objections in turn.

Hillerdal presents his first objection in a rather peculiar guise, noting that my analysis cannot count on gaining general philosophical support, and referring to the fact that I myself realize that my analysis is in conflict with antimetaphysical philosophy. This is all true, but I fail to see how it can constitute an objection. No philosophical analysis can count on gaining general philosophical support. With my analysis I lay claim to practicing philosophy, which means I am prepared to be contradicted philosophically and to contradict the philosophy of others—in short, to dispute about what is philosophically right. But I do not lay claim to taking the exceptional philosophical position of presenting an analysis that is supposedly sure of general recognition "with the state of today's philosophical debate." (And incidentally, is there not something missing in that phrase? Should it not have read: "with the state of today's philosophical debate—in Sweden, or in Scandinavia, or in the Anglo-Saxon world"?) Never before have the philosophical issues been so far removed from one another, indeed so irrelevant to one another, as is the case today between philosophy in the Anglo-Saxon world (including Scandinavia) and philosophy on the European continent. Therefore, today more than ever, it is futile to argue against an analysis by saying that it cannot count on general recognition. The truth of the matter is, there is not a single claim within philosophical ethics on which consensus reigns.

Hillerdal also presents his objection in another guise I find strange, asserting that I have a philosophical view that I have turned into the philosophy *par préférence.* Why, Hillerdal has done exactly the same thing, except for making the antimetaphysical philosophy and its emotive value theory his ethical philosophy of choice.

No, we must let go of all this—both the question as to whether our philosophical analyses are recognized as universally valid or not, and the question as to whether we have a philosophy *par préférence* or not—and, instead, dispute about the real issue. I have done so earlier in this rejoinder in my attempt to show that Hillerdal's critique of my analysis of the relationship of trust does not hold true, because his antimetaphysical philosophy causes him to simplify the issue.

But now to the second argument Hillerdal levels against me, which is that my philosophical analysis is suspiciously well suited to Christianity's view of ethical matters. I cannot see why there should necessarily be anything wrong with that. But it rests on the fact that Hillerdal and I do not agree on Christianity's view of ethical matters.

Since the contents of the gospel are what no human being could have foreseen, the gospel has no relation to philosophy. One cannot, however, deduce from this that the law—the ethical demand—has no relation to philosophy. On the contrary, since the law is universal, to stay with Wingren's expression, it must have to do with philosophy. In other words, one cannot jointly determine the gospel's and the law's relation to philosophy. Rather, the question must be asked separately for the gospel and for the law. But Hillerdal does not do this. He lets the law's relation to philosophy be determined along with the gospel's relation to philosophy, and in this I cannot follow him. The gospel is historical, the law universal, and Hillerdal ignores this crucial difference. The law, or the ethical demand, is given with life as it happens to be. The gospel, the message of God's forgiveness, is given historically with Jesus of Nazareth. A confrontation cannot be arranged unless one has a common cause, and philosophy and theology have that with regard to the law and to creation, but not with regard to the gospel. And because Hillerdal has not formed a clear picture of which aspects of the Christian faith's content are historical and which are universal, he can let the relationship between philosophical and theological ethics be based on the relationship between revelation and reason.

In other words, there is something in Christianity that is not accessible to phenomenological analysis, namely, everything in it that is unforeseen, and there is something in Christianity that is accessible to phenomenological analysis thanks to its universality, namely the ethical demand, the law. Therefore, if the philosophical analysis of the ethical demand corresponds to Christianity's understanding of the law, then surely this fact does not speak against the philosophical correctness of the philosophical analysis to anyone who regards Christianity as the truth about life.

In his concluding chapter concerning the independence of theological ethics, Hillerdal claims that because it counts on "revelation," theological ethics does not have to do with the same reality as the reality philosophy is intended to describe and investigate. In so doing, however, he is posing the problem much too summarily. As far as theology deals with that which is universal in Christianity, theology has to do with the same reality as philosophy. Here we therefore run into a real clash, a dispute about the right analysis in philosophical terms, and not merely (as Hillerdal seeks to limit it to) a theological analysis of philosophical ethics as an important cultural phenomenon (*Teologisk og filosofisk etik,* 237–238). But Hillerdal and I apparently disagree on the scope of philosophy. I believe that ontological, and also fundamentally ontological, problems belong within philosophy, just as they also belong within theology.

And let me add yet another consideration. I utterly fail to see how it should be "demeaning" for a philosopher to let himself be inspired by theologians. I cannot see anything wrong in an existential philosopher being inspired by Kierkegaard, as Hillerdal notes—or by Luther and Augustine, he might have added. If what Hillerdal claims is true, namely, that existential philosophy is, to a great extent, very suitable as an interpretation of Luther's teachings concerning the things already demanded by "the natural law," then certainly it indicates that this philosophy is philosophically right—provided, that is, that the law Luther speaks of is indeed natural (universal).

Hillerdal finds it philosophically dubious that existential philosophy can only be accepted in a Christian environment, but will hardly be accepted in an environment defined by Hinduism or secularized Buddhism. But is it an ideal, then, to purge philosophy of all the interesting and crucial issues? To make it so un-ontological that it can be coupled with any proclamation?

4. Understanding and decision

In an essay entitled "Relativismens problem" (The Problem of Relativism), which appeared in his book *Med syvtallet* (With the Seven) (Copenhagen, 1959), Professor Lomholt deals with the relationship between understanding and decision. On the subject of decisions, he sees me as wanting to get some solid ground under my feet, or, in other words, he believes that I seek to understand as much as possible in order to decide as little as possible. Lomholt finds this motivation to be evident in two places: in my emphasis on the significance of tradition and in my distancing myself from Kierkegaard's making the understanding be won in, and by virtue of, the decision.

In response to the question of what the tendency that Lomholt finds in my work, namely, the tendency to take from the decision to add to the understanding, has to do with the problem of relativism, the reply is that tradition does not suffice, but fails. And because of this failure of tradition, which renders us unable to find the understanding that was meant to reduce the risk of the decision, we are faced with the problem of relativism. Consequently, we—along with Kierkegaard—are obliged to win the understanding in, and by virtue of, the decision. We cannot come to grips with the problem of relativism through understanding, for there is no understanding; tradition cannot supply us with it, for it is too deceitful for that. The problem of relativism therefore persists, imbuing our decisions with all the risk that comes from inadequate understanding.

I shall address the question of tradition first. As I said, Lomholt finds that, driven by a wish to gain security, I have emphasized its importance far too much, even going so far as to risk leaving no room for heretics and rebels in my ethics, although he does concede I have given them ample room in my historical presentation. One is, of course, placed in a rather difficult situation in a debate when one is attacked on the grounds of one's motivations. It seems anything but credible for a debater to solemnly state that he certainly never had the motives attributed to him, because in the interest of fairness it must be conceded that quite often we ourselves are the last to know what our motives were. I shall therefore refrain from denying Lomholt's claim, but observe in all modesty that in emphasizing the significance of tradition, I am conscious of only one thing, which is the following: Much of the continental philosophy of the nineteenth and early twentieth centuries—which was epistemologically oriented—spoke and thought about human beings as if they were subjects devoid of history and tradition. However, the recognition that human beings live historically has typically become central to the considerations of the philosophy of our time, and along with it the understanding of the significance of tradition. Naturally, I too have come under the influence of this latter philosophy. To the best of my knowledge I emphasize tradition for no other reason than that I was once under the influence of the older philosophy, which ignored its significance. My fellow undergraduates and I were still schooled in that philosophy.

But now, on to my disagreement with Kierkegaard. Initially I have to say that to contrast decisions in which understanding exists beforehand with decisions in which everything is incomprehensible beforehand is to frame the problem too crudely—something of which I, too, have been guilty. If there is not a certain understanding as to what the decision is about, then of course there is no decision. Yet a person's understanding can be too inadequate to yield any certainty beforehand about whether the decision one is making is the right decision. Arguably, this alone can be the meaning of saying the understanding is only won in, and by virtue of, the decision. Let us consider a decision such as choosing one's profession in life. Naturally, everyone will have a certain understanding of what this decision is about: they will know something about what the relevant profession consists in, and they will also know something about their own inclinations and skills. However, their knowledge of the conditions of that profession may be quite theoretical or abstract, their inclinations may change, and they may have little more than a vague idea of whether their skills will be adequate or not. To put it briefly, a person's understanding of what this decision is about rests to a considerable degree on the deceitful understanding of their imagination. But a decision must be made, and so we make it, and not until that decision has placed us in our chosen profession do we learn either that the decision was right or that it was wrong. Or perhaps we never find out for certain whether it was right or wrong.

I do deny, however, that it is always the case that understanding and certainty reduce the risk of the decision, and that a failure to understand and a lack of certainty increase the risk: there are other types of risks than that of one's decision proving to be wrong. There is, for instance, the risk that someone might lose their life in the enterprise they become involved in—a risk not unknown in our century. Everything may have been laid open to the light of day, all the consequences may have been taken into consideration, understanding may be complete, without all this making the risk even the tiniest bit smaller. The danger connected with the action remains equally great.

So two types of risk exist. There are decisions where nothing is lacking in the understanding of what one is getting into, so that the risk belongs to the action and its consequences. Then there are decisions where, due to a lack of understanding, the risk consists in the decision proving to be wrong.

What I oppose is pronouncing the decision where the risk belongs to the decision itself to be the only genuine decision. The reason given for such a claim does not hold true. It is not correct that a decision must be devoid of understanding and uncertain in itself for the person to be wholly committed. Even a decision based on an adequate understanding of where one will end up as a result of the decision—so that the risk belongs to the action and its consequences—can sometimes demand that someone becomes wholly and personally committed.

Of course we cannot eradicate from our lives the uncertainty that springs from our lack of understanding, since our understanding is, and remains, lacking. But I do not see this as a reason for cultivating uncertainty. I agree with Lomholt that a decision of this nature was at issue for Kierkegaard, and that the same types of decisions often become an issue in connection with illness, but that does not make them more genuine as decisions than the ones in which the risk belongs to the action and its consequences. Should one not in all cases at least seek to obtain an understanding that is as comprehensive and as detailed as possible, not only in relation to ethical-political decisions (of which I mentioned examples in my essay on "The Ethical Choice"),[2] but also in relation to more ethical-existential decisions (such as the choice of profession) and to decisions in which the ethical-political and ethical-existential questions intermingle (as exemplified by the citizen for whom the government's subjugation of his fellow citizens raises the question of whether it is time to conspire and prepare for revolution)? One should wish that the decision one reaches involves as little as possible of the risk that springs from the failure of self-understanding, or from the inadequacy of one's understanding of the relevant context. I concede that I find it best if no one doubts whether the decision they have reached was the right one, provided their certainty is not due to narrow-mindedness. There is really more than enough risk to spare as it is. There is ample risk connected with the decision in which understanding is no problem because I know what is right in the ethical-political sense and have no doubts as to my ethical-existential duty, but in which everything depends on will because I am extremely loath to do it.

Let me add just one thing. Lomholt says: "Kierkegaard did not reject the decision in which it is established in advance what is true. He was just as eager to be able to arrive at this decision as Løgstrup is. But there were certain reasons why he was unable to arrive at this decision." Lomholt is probably right. But I am also right when I claim that Kierkegaard opted for the decisions in which an understanding is only won in, and by virtue of, the decision. But how can Lomholt and I both be right when our claims are contradictory? Well, the reason is that we each read Kierkegaard in our own way. Lomholt reads him from an individual-psychological point of view, while I read him from a philosophical point of view. I do not say this, as it is commonly done, to play off the two ways of reading Kierkegaard against one another, for neither way is well served by being isolated from the other. But for the time being, all I would like to do is to claim that the individual-psychological reasons, which prevented Kierkegaard from arriving at the decision in which the truth is established in advance (as Lomholt expresses it), caused him to make the philosophical claim that the genuine decision is the one in which understanding is only won in, and by virtue of, the decision. Kierkegaard is used in existentialist philosophy and existentialist theology to claim that the decision requiring a person to be wholly committed only exists where the understanding is won by virtue of the decision alone—and that use of Kierkegaard is not wrong, for Kierkegaard already used himself in that way.

I do not deny that we have to deal with decisions whose uncertainty, because understanding evades us, require people to commit themselves wholly, and I regard it as the achievement and merit of existentialist theology that it insists these decisions are an inevitable part of the conditions of our lives. But I do deny that only that type of decision requires people to wholly commit themselves, and I deny that only such decisions are genuine, with the result that seeking to understand should be regarded as a dubious undertaking.

5. Misfortune—suffering

I have now come to a complex of problems relating to a certain point on which Stangerup has interpreted me in a manner I find both unpleasant and surprising. Since he is not alone in doing so, however, I have probably expressed myself too succinctly. Allow me to briefly clarify how I meant this point to be understood. I have spoken of the protest in the name of suffering against the idea of life being a gift, and my intention in doing so was to concede that there is a limit to the line of reasoning I have attempted to pursue. Here this line of reasoning is contradicted, and that contradiction is impossible for me to do away with. My purpose in claiming that there is "a world of difference between . . . the suffering of physical and mental illness which one must bear alone"[3] and the despair over death was to say that we cannot get rid of the fact that suffering leads us to question life's being a gift. I did not go on to disavow what I had just said and to claim that a person who is ill was never alone with his suffering, but that other people were always a part of the suffering person's life, and were a part of it in such a way that they were essential to him, so that the idea that life had been given him as a gift could not be foreign to him, in spite of his situation. But I did go on to say: "If the illness hinders the development of a person's abilities and powers, if the pain prevents him or her from entering into the experiences of life, other people must supply an indispensable and living part of his or her existence if life in its character of something received as a gift is to hold its own through all the suffering." I expressed myself hypothetically, implying: "otherwise it cannot." I expressed myself hypothetically because we all know that very often there are no other people to supply an indispensable and living part in the life of a suffering person, and in that case, life cannot hold its own as a gift.

Another thing may also have played a role in the way I have been interpreted. I do not know, but let me at least present the problem. The approach most people are inclined to take when reading a systematic work, and which the systematists themselves usually encourage, is to regard this work as expressing a position. This means that it professes to offer the reader views that are capable, like beams of light, of sweeping full circle around the horizon, shedding light on all the issues. Admittedly the author himself has not been everywhere, but readers can extrapolate on their own. That can also account for the odd imbalance that often occurs between, on the one hand, the grand, intricate conceptual apparatus occupying most of the available space, and, on the other, the sparse, scattered information about concrete situations—bearing in mind that the former was, after all, meant only to serve the latter. In my work I have aspired to the opposite, which is the basis for the important role I have attributed to the phenomenological analyses. My book is a monograph, and nothing more. The views I have presented cannot be used to elucidate any other problems than the ones I have used them to elucidate. New problems demand new views (and new phenomenological analyses).

Stangerup goes on to say that if there is even a single person "for whom life is a curse, this one person is an insult to, indeed a scandal for, *The Ethical Demand*." That is not true, however. It would only be true if I had professed to offer a system in which all the contradictions, of which our life is full, were supposed to be annulled. But I have not done so. It is true that there is suffering that questions and contradicts the idea that life is a gift, but this suffering does not invalidate the idea. Just because things are irreconcilable and cannot be harmonized, it does not mean they annihilate each other. They remain as a contradiction. And let me add that no philosopher or theologian has presented a solution to the problem of suffering, so if the fact that the problem remains unsolved is fatal to my lines of reasoning, then it is fatal to all philosophy and theology.

Stangerup argues his view based on the axiom "all or nothing." Either life is good, and in that case everything must be good and there must be no suffering, or else there is suffering, and in that case everything is evil and there is nothing good about life. But that is not establishing what life is. On the contrary, it is demanding of life that life should be a certain way. Stangerup demands of life's own goodness that, if it really is goodness, it has to be goodness in such an all-encompassing sense that there must be no suffering at all. Life does not fulfill this demand, so Stangerup refuses to recognize the goodness as goodness. Stangerup wants no contradiction: it must be done away with completely, and therefore in the name of suffering he eradicates life's own goodness—not only for the suffering person, but for everyone. Naturally this is not a description of Stangerup's general outlook, but only a description of the view that is crucial to his argument on this point.

Professor Søe, too, finds this particular passage in my work "hopelessly unsatisfactory," noting in this connection: "Scores of people are certainly not full of gratitude for life's peculiarities. Pessimism and existential melancholy are not just isolated, passing phenomena, and not known only from the lives of those who are especially devastated by suffering and hardship." And Søe asks: "Incidentally, was Karl Barth completely wrong when he once said that were it not for Christ, one might just as well regard life on earth as a sort of 'forecourt to Hell'?"

To this I would reply: Karl Barth was not right. Of course the experience of absurdity, to speak in Camus' phraseology, cannot be debated away. The question is, however, whether the experience of absurdity is at all possible without maintaining, as a precondition, the basic idea that life is given as a gift to the individual. Is it not precisely because life is worth living—because life is good—that people groan and complain and accuse life when it nevertheless turns out to be so absurd?

What is the nature of the experience of absurdity? Is it the experience that life is never anything but evil, misfortune, suffering, and emptiness? Or is it the experience that people are cheated out of the life that is a gift of goodness to those who have received it? I believe the latter. Where else would people have got the idea of the goodness, happiness, and fulfillment against which they measure absurdity if not from their own existence, from their own lives with other people, from their minds being nourished and healed by the world and things as they are? The greater the rebellion involved in the experience of absurdity, the more alive is the thought that life is created and given as a gift—alive in the negation of its givenness. The rebellion in the experience of absurdity gains its passion from the life that was created and given. Absolute nihilism is an impossibility.

Peter Kemp, who touches upon the same issues as Søe and Stangerup in his book *Person og tænkning* (Person and Thinking) (Copenhagen, 1960), asks me whether the proclamation of the gospel is not "the only thing we can do in the face of pessimism?" (168). I am, however, unable to acknowledge the question. The gospel speaks to guilt, not to pessimism. At any rate, the gospel speaks to pessimism only insofar as that pessimism is based on an unwillingness to face up to one's guilt.

As I see it, there are only two alternatives: the view of existentialist theology, and my view. As far as I can see, the demand as a radical demand arises out of life's own goodness, out of—let me just put it this way—the joy of existing; for in this joy, life is experienced as given to us. Suffering, misfortune, bear witness against it. Thus, both happiness and misfortune have to do with the question of whether our life is given to us, and therefore also have to do with the question of the radicality and one-sidedness of the demand. As a consequence of this, we cannot avoid the contradiction inherent in our existence.

The other alternative is that of existentialist theology, clearly and consistently carried through by Olesen Larsen. This view insists upon the Kierkegaardian contrast between suffering and misfortune. What I have referred to above as "suffering" is referred to as "misfortune" in this context, since suffering is assigned a religious sense. Suffering is construed as "dying away from the world," not finding one's life's fulfillment in anything the world has to offer, but instead existing only for God. Misfortune is construed as everything that befalls a person in his or her life in the world, not least mental and physical illness. Suffering consists in—religiously—renouncing the possibility of finding one's life's fulfillment in anything the world has to offer. Misfortune consists in being afflicted by external factors and hindered in one's still-living and immediate wish to have one's life fulfilled by the things the world has to give. Misfortune does not challenge the idea that life is given as a gift to the individual, for that idea has nothing to do with life's own goodness and happiness. There is nothing in our existence, such as it immediately is, that has anything to do with whether our life is a gift or not. Happiness does not bear witness to it; misfortune does not bear witness against it. The life of any individual is only given through their faith in God, not outside of it. The ethical demand therefore has nothing to do with our life's own goodness, but belongs exclusively to the individual's relation to God and consists in God's demand that the individual die away from the world. This, and this alone, is what the demand's radicality consists in. Hence, misfortune's contradiction of the idea that life is a gift does not exist in the theology inspired by Kierkegaard, either.

I see no alternatives apart from these two. Either one finds that life's own goodness helps suggest that life is a gift given to the individual but is contradicted by misfortune—choosing to leave the contradiction standing—or one is bound to claim, along with existentialist theology, that seeing the merest connection between the ethical demand and the understanding of life as a gift is a way of avoiding the demand of dying away from the world in one's faith in God, which is the only radical demand.

Lomholt also criticizes my views on this point. It is true, he says, that life is a gift, inasmuch as that means we are put under an obligation by it, and that we assume guilt. "That we have been granted life, that we have been put into it, that it has been given to us, no one would ever attempt to deny that. Or to put it differently, no one has ever come across a human being who did not feel guilt." It does not do, however, to speak as I do of life being a gift, something given to us. Whether one's life has been a gift or not depends, Lomholt says, on what good fortune life has bestowed upon one, and what misfortunes one has been afflicted with—and if one allows the ethical demand to be given through life's being a gift, then it comes to depend upon one's good fortune and misfortune. Furthermore, referring to my statement that for one on whom fate has smiled, it can be true that life is a gift, Lomholt says: "I should think that determining whether fate has smiled upon one is impossible until the course of life has been run. Does that mean, then, that one must at least have come in a decent second before one is able to decide whether the idea of understanding life as something of a bequest or a gift can be true?"

Lomholt's objection is, in effect, threefold. He objects that if the demand is given through life's being a gift, it does not apply to someone who has known nothing but misfortune. He also objects that the demand is graduated depending on the amount of good fortune with which each of us is endowed. Finally, he objects that one must await the completion of life before being able to know anything of what the demand was about, since no one can know their fate until then.

Let me begin by considering Lomholt's last objection. An observation such as the one that the course must have been completed before anyone can say whether fate has smiled upon them belongs within the ethic of Aristotle, in which the good is *eudaimonia,* understood as the flourishing life, and the observation is in fact found there. Lomholt is right in saying that it would be fatal for my argument if Aristotelian considerations were a consequence of it—which Lomholt believes they are, given that fate must have smiled upon a person in order for the demand to apply to him or her. I must say I do not agree with Lomholt on this point. Allow me to give a harsh example: The things demanded of a German Jew as a young or middle-aged man and trusted employee, living comfortably and safely within the Wilhelmian bourgeoisie, were very different from the things demanded of him when, as an old man, thrown out of his position, he lived a life of persecution until he was killed. Yet surely the persecution did not retrogradely rescind the demands to which he was subjected, and which he lived up to while he was not persecuted.

Nor can I say it is an objection that the demand is graduated. "From everyone to whom much has been given, much will be required; and from one to whom much has been entrusted, even more will be demanded." In the parable of the talents, in which one servant was given five talents, another servant two, and a third servant one, it might be reasonable to say that the servant who got two talents came in a decent second.

This still leaves the first objection, which is, of course, the crucial one. I admit that the problem exists, and that I cannot solve it. Why, then (Lomholt will probably ask me), do I not subscribe to the view of Kierkegaard and existentialist theology: that good fortune and misfortune have nothing whatsoever to do with ethics? Because if I do, the radical demand becomes unconnected with our existence such as it actually is. It becomes abstract. He who gives the demand becomes another than he who creates our existence. And with what must the demand be obeyed? Certainly with that which a person is given.

I willingly admit that in the proclamation of Jesus—and here I am thinking of his ethical proclamation, which is not rooted in his eschatological message—no emphasis is placed on the demand being obeyed with that which a person is given. But I would imagine that this is because it went without saying. The worldview in which Jesus and his followers were steeped was neither atheistic nor nihilistic, but determined by the Jewish belief that the world had been created by God.

In one of the passages where Jesus intensifies the law of the Old Testament, he refers to the gifts from God of which life is composed as the reason for this procedure. I am thinking of the passage: "You have heard that it was said, 'You shall love your neighbor and hate your enemy.' But I say to you, Love your enemies and pray for those who persecute you, so that you may be children of your Father in heaven; for he makes his sun rise on the evil and on the good, and sends rain on the righteous and on the unrighteous." This passage does not emphasize, either, that the demand be obeyed with the gifts we receive. The emphasis lies elsewhere. It lies in the acknowledgment that just as everything joyful in our existence— sun and rain—is allotted to us, regardless of whether we deserve it or not, that is how we ought to love our neighbor, regardless of whether this neighbor is our friend or our enemy. Yet even so, that does not preclude—on the contrary it presupposes—that the demand must be obeyed with the gifts, sun and rain, that are allotted to us. Otherwise the talk about God letting his sun rise on the good and the evil and his rain fall on the righteous and unrighteous is reduced to a randomly chosen illustration of our neighbor being both our friend and our enemy. Our existence is reduced, not only to the random and essentially inconsequential circumstances under which the demand must be obeyed; it is also reduced to a source of metaphors and pictures of what the demand is about.

I realize that the reasoning I have set out here does not resolve the problem presented in Lomholt's objection: Should unfortunate people not also obey the demand with their misfortune? Those whom misfortune has prevented from enjoying sun and rain, and who cannot obey the demand with their pleasure in the sun and the rain—should not they, too, obey the demand with their misfortune?

6. Is there a Christian ethic?

Stangerup prefers Christian ethics to human ethics, and gives the following reason: "At least *this* [namely, a Christian ethic] knows it is surely better to maintain certain requirements that can be of tremendous value to those who really have not been endowed with ethical and pedagogical talent, and who therefore need guidelines that are straight and clear."

In my view, however, that way of understanding the difference between human and Christian ethics is imaginary. It is as though advocating human ethics were tantamount to renouncing straight, clear guidelines and simply propagandizing in favor of uncertainty, and as though Christian ethics consisted solely of incontestable requirements that people can simply adhere to. Actually, the human ethicist can speak with great certainty, and does so. Claiming that Christian ethics is to be preferred because of some ability to provide incontestable guidance simply goes against all the facts. Two examples will clearly illustrate this. Let us imagine a married couple who cannot have children, and who suffer on that account. They consider artificial insemination, but in their case the only option is to use a heterogeneous donor. They ask themselves: is this justifiable? They seek guidance in Christian ethics, reading Professor Søe, who took the very commendable step some years ago of approaching such a difficult problem, thinking it through, and presenting his opinion on it. I shall not reproduce his considerations here. Suffice it to say that Professor Søe would not rule out artificial insemination using a heterogeneous donor. Imagine, then, that our couple are German—Professor Søe being widely read in Germany—and that they also subscribe to the periodical *Evangelische Ethik* (Evangelical Ethics). They may well read an article on the same subject, in the issue dated 1 February 1958, written by the well-known Dutch theologian Dr. Bloemhof, in which he vehemently condemns Professor Søe's view, and does so by invoking precisely the same theology as Professor Søe invokes, namely a modified Barthianism. And now I ask: what about the Christian ethic's upholding of requirements "that can be of tremendous value to those who really have not been endowed with ethical and pedagogical talent"? To whom should they listen, Professor Søe or Dr. Bloemhof?

Now for the second example. In his work *Kristelig etik* (Christian Ethics), Professor Søe expresses the wish that we might have Christian politicians. But was Søe pleased, I wonder, at having his wish fulfilled during the years Foster Dulles controlled America's foreign policy?

No, it is not possible to distinguish between human and Christian ethics in the way that Stangerup does.

At this point I find it appropriate to move on to a discussion with Professor Søe, who believes there is an applied Christian ethic just as adamantly as I deny it—an "applied ethic" being understood as an ethic that takes a position on concrete ethical questions. And I will begin by asking: What does it actually mean when we say an applied ethic is Christian? I ask because there are two different interpretations.

Is the meaning that in the Christian message we find guidance and instructions that point to the appropriate solution to an ethical problem for the Christian, but do not concern the non-Christian because the solution in question presupposes faith in the Christian message? If this is the meaning, an applied Christian ethic can only play host to the type of decisions in which the individual acts on his own behalf, whereas all decisions in which the individual acts on behalf of others fall outside its scope. Imagine, for the sake of example, an applied Christian ethic that rigorously precludes divorce—as Catholic applied ethics does with reference to the sacramental status of marriage, and as Protestant applied ethics has often done with reference to suffering belonging to the Christian's life in vocation. Because we are dealing here with decisions made by the individual Christian on his or her own behalf, they can be a theme in an applied Christian ethic. Political decisions, on the other hand, could not be treated in such applied Christian ethics, as they are made on behalf of other people, both Christians and non-Christians. The Christian politician would not be able to find any guidance in his applied Christian ethic for drawing up a divorce law, for instance, as such a law would have to concern all people, regardless of whether they believe the Christian message or not. Let us refer to this type of applied Christian ethic as *partial*.

An applied Christian ethic could also be interpreted as something else, however: as the view that certainly Christians and non-Christians are subject to the same requirements, but only by incorporating the Christian message can anyone be truly or fully enlightened as to the meaning of these requirements. Common ethical guidance for Christians and non-Christians can best be had, or perhaps only be had, from Christianity. If this is the case, then the radical ethical demand must also concern the non-Christian, for without it, according to the same applied Christian ethic, we cannot arrive at the right solutions to the concrete ethical problems. In other words, the ethical demand does not require the Christian message of God's forgiveness to make it radical. In this second interpretation, an applied Christian ethic would also be able to deal with political problems, and we could refer to it as *universal*.

Which type of applied Christian ethic does Professor Søe advocate? Well, that depends on his view of the ethical demand. If he regards it as concerning everyone, then the applied Christian ethic is universal; if he regards it as concerning only Christians, then the applied Christian ethic becomes partial. But what is Søe's view of the ethical demand? Of this there can be no doubt.

As for my claim that the ethical demand in its radicality is not a particularly Christian demand, Søe polemicizes against it, and with considerable vigor. He is "completely astounded" at my account. He says that I will not get one single person who is not a Christian to agree with it. No one "save a Christian theologian could ever think of saying something like that." Søe invokes the non-Christians, who will certainly find that here I have "risen too high." "They will say something to the effect that our self-assertion and desire to get ahead . . . do, as a matter of course, have their own justification, but that we must remember not to tread on others too brutally. And of course, most nice people will admit that we are probably more prone to err in favor of self-assertion. But people will not treat these drawbacks as high tragedy, although they will hope that by and large, these aspects will be offset by 'exceedingly' unselfish actions." And then—I think I should be allowed the liberty of interpreting Søe this way—the non-Christian basically has just cause, for the radical nature of the demand presupposes faith in God's unfathomable forgiveness, and since the non-Christian does not hold that faith, he cannot accept a demand as radical, either. Consequently, as for all my explanations about how the radical demand is heard "before, and independently of, the revelation of Christ," Søe "eradicates" them or brands them "as totally and completely unsatisfactory."

However, if this decisive difference in the way Christians and non-Christians perceive ethical issues does exist, as Søe believes, then it follows that Christians and non-Christians cannot have a common applied ethic; the applied Christian ethic, which Søe advocates, can only be an ethic for Christians. This in turn must mean that all the ethical-political problems calling for solutions that concern non-Christians and Christians alike, and doing so precisely because of their political nature, cannot have a place within applied Christian ethics. But does Søe draw this conclusion?

To exemplify his claim that the ethical demand is a particularly Christian demand, Søe uses the parable of the good Samaritan, referring to its ability to break down all national and religious barriers for love of one's neighbor. I must say, however, that to me precisely this parable seems to exemplify the part of Christ's ethical proclamation that is not rooted in his eschatological message, but in which he formulates and articulates the universal demand of loving one's neighbor that applies to every human being. In this same connection, Søe believes it was correct that a particularly Christian justification was given, or as Søe expresses it, that a "Christian 'no' to Hitler's Jewish laws and the Nazis' conduct towards the Jews" was given. I would have preferred the justification to be human and not Christian. Unlike Søe, I regard it as a Christian claim that the ethical demand is not a specifically Christian demand. Thus, Christians should not fight their own battle in situations where Christians and non-Christians have a common battle to fight, for if they do, then in the eyes of Christian faith the Christians thereby deny that the ethical demand is universal. Incidentally, this stance can easily, although not necessarily, lead the Christians to refrain from taking any action until the church is disturbed, and not before. History—even recent history—bears witness to this. But I would also mention an example of the opposite. The greatest civic problem that my generation of Danes has faced may well have been the Criminal Law Amendment Act of 1 June 1945.[4] The fact that it was a theologian, namely H. Østergaard-Nielsen, who wrote the first and best contribution to the debate was a coincidence. It was no coincidence, however, that this theologian did not present any theological justification for his analysis and protest. Had he wished to do so, his contribution could not possibly have been as good as it was, and it would probably also have come tagging along far behind.

I do not believe that an applied Christian ethic is possible, either in a partial or in a universal version. That is not to say a theologian who subscribes to an applied Christian ethic is unable to present excellent reflections concerning ethical problems of one sort and another. All I mean is that, in reality, his strictly human reflections are what prove decisive and that he lets himself fall prey to an illusion when he says it is the Christian message. Søe finds my following statement completely unreasonable: "To try to make a case in the matter of political and ethical questions by appealing to the Christian message always leads to an oversimplification of the problems whereby the decisive considerations are lost sight of altogether." I certainly admit that this pronouncement could benefit from some modification. Let me therefore formulate my idea in the following, more adequate, manner: If an adherent of applied Christian ethics were to deduce his perception of political and ethical questions from the Christian message, then he would lose sight of all decisive reflections. When this does not happen, the reason is that, without knowing it himself, he is actually arguing his case in strictly human terms.

Peter Kemp says that in ethical questions it is reasonable to seek guidance in history from theologians and humanists, and that we actually do so. This is true enough, but it does not decide the question of whether there is an applied Christian ethic or not. In his treatment of this or that ethical problem, a modern ethicist can very well allow himself to be guided by the theologians of the past, all the way back to the authors of the New

Testament, without this necessarily meaning that he subscribes to an applied Christian ethic. He does not do so until he believes there are solutions to ethical problems which—whether they concern Christians alone, or Christians and non-Christians alike—cannot be justified in human terms, but only in Christian terms.

Hillerdal also takes issue with my rejection of a Christian ethic, both in the publication already mentioned and in his *Kyrka och socialetik* (Church and Social Ethics) (1960). According to him, one of the consequences of this rejection is that I come to ignore The Great Commission to preach the gospel. That is true enough, but it is no objection. One must be able to set oneself a limited task, and the sole question is whether any of the things I have said in human terms has been rendered false because something else has been omitted. And as far as the question of confession, proclamation, and mission is concerned, this question lies beyond the problem of whether an applied Christian ethic does or does not exist.

Hillerdal does, in fact, admit that I have posed myself the limited task of giving "a definition in strictly human terms of the relationship to the other person which is contained within the religious proclamation of Jesus of Nazareth." Nevertheless—he objects—I move from this task to that of rebuffing all specifically Christian ethics. And that will not do, for, as he says, the New Testament also contains Paul's theology and the other letters, as well as Revelation and the Acts of the Apostles. Thus, I have failed to provide evidence that no special Christian ethic can be based on that part of the New Testament either (*Teologisk og filosofisk etik,* 172 and 263).

This is naturally correct, but I doubt that an investigation would change my view. Allow me to assert just one thing: The ethical proclamation made by Jesus of God's universal demand, as we know it from the first three Gospels, is not found in Paul, nor is it found in the scriptures attributed to John. They do speak of loving one's neighbor, but that love is Christologically based, and the way Jesus spoke of it was lost. But this I regard as a deficiency in the proclamations of Paul and John.

Hillerdal furthermore disagrees with my interpretation of the proclamation of Jesus, as we know it from the first three Gospels. He objects that I disregard the passages that emphasize the messianic awareness of Jesus.

It is clear to me that Hillerdal and I take different views of which elements in the Gospels go back to Jesus Christ's own proclamation, and which must be attributed to the reshaping and additions of the congregation. A number of the texts that Hillerdal attributes to Jesus, I attribute to the congregation. Looking beyond that issue, however, one must distinguish between two questions. First: Did Jesus himself think he spoke on God's behalf? Did he think that with his own message God's kingdom was coming? The answer must be "yes." He not only spoke *about* God's kingdom, but was certain that God made his words and works into God's own words and works. Next: Did Jesus also proclaim what his own life and death meant for the coming of God's kingdom? I believe the answer to this must be "no." Preaching this was reserved for his disciples.

Hillerdal does not distinguish between these two questions (*Teologisk og filosofisk etik,* 15). When Hillerdal asserts that the Sermon on the Mount is to be understood as the Son of God, the Savior of the world, speaking, he gives us no clue as to whether Jesus says what he says in the Sermon on the basis of this self-understanding, or whether it is based on the disciples' understanding of Jesus. If one fails to keep the two questions separate, however, one comes to give the proclamation of Jesus a theologically reflected accent which is foreign to it, and which is out of place.

7. The unfulfillability of the demand

In an article in the Stockholm *Dagens Nyheter* (Daily News), Ulla Åhgren deals with the contradiction in which, I believe, we find ourselves ethically, namely, that it is inherent in the ethical demand that it claims to be fulfillable and that, considering our nature, it is unfulfillable. If we adhere to the assumption that our nature makes the demand unfulfillable, then we remove all gravity from the demand. If we agree with the demand's claim that it is fulfillable, we allow ourselves to fall prey to illusions about our own nature. It is through this contradiction a person hears the Christian message and believes in its forgiveness, and assumes the unfulfillability as his or her guilt.

Ulla Åhgren presents two objections. That which is impossible on the human level must also be impossible on the religious level. If, on the human level, regarding the demand as fulfillable leads to self-deception, in which we fall prey to illusions about our own nature, it must lead to self-deception on the religious level as well. Ulla Åhgren is right in this observation. Actual human nature does not become something different by virtue of a person believing the Christian message, and the contradiction therefore remains at the religious level. I would just like to add that the character of the contradiction is changed, because something is added with the Christian message. The Christian message does not solely take into account what a person actually is, but also takes into account what a person is in light of the message: a forgiven human being. At this point, the contradiction consists in the fact that individuals do not live and act on the basis of what they are in light of the message in which they believe, but persist in living and acting on the basis of their actual nature and therefore continuously reduce to theory that which should be belief.

The second objection Ulla Åhgren presents is that my perception of human nature is much too firmly fixed. Human nature is not given once and for all, but varies with environment. Here, however, I believe we must distinguish, depending on the light in which we view human nature. If we view it in light of the social norms, the moral, legal, and conventional demands, then human nature is changeable and can be made to vary in different environments. On the other hand, if we view it in light of the radical demand, human nature is invariable. Ulla Åhgren broaches this herself when she says that what applies to "phenomena on the level of rights and duties" may not "touch upon the most important area; what is good and evil."

In a later article, Ulla Åhgren refers to my account of natural love being neither selfish nor unselfish because the other person belongs to one's own world in such a way that the consideration for the other person and for oneself coincide. And she continues: If the command given to us, that we should love our neighbor, is about us loving all others (strangers and enemies included) as naturally as we otherwise love our nearest and dearest, then the astonishing consequence is that if this command were obeyed, the difference between egoism and altruism would become nonexistent, and there would no longer be any possibility of acting unselfishly. Ulla Åhgren is right in saying that this would be the consequence—a consequence I acknowledge. It supports my view, for the consequence involves the recognition that morality does not exist for its own sake. Nor does the radical demand. This I have expressed as follows: What is demanded is that the demand ought not to have been necessary. Therein consists its radicality.

Peter Kemp protests against my saying that the radical demand is unfulfillable. The demand is fulfilled, he claims, when it has an effect in a person's life without that person's knowledge.

To this I would say that if we ourselves are to be suspended in order for the demand to be, not obeyed, but able to have an effect, then the demand will hardly be fulfillable. I do not think it is too much to say that Kemp suspends the self, for he inquires, "But why, then, do we not always fulfill the demand?" and he replies, "Well, simply because the ultimate authority does not always perform the deeds of love" (*Person og tænkning*, 179).[5] But then it becomes the ultimate authority's fault and not mine that I do not do good deeds. Therefore the following explanation is concerned with using a method of elimination to lay the guilt upon human beings: since we cannot lay the guilt upon God (since that would make us begin to speculate), it must consequently be laid upon humans.

I believe it really would be more adequate to settle for saying that in the life of a human being there exist immediate realities such as trust and love, which are on the side of the ethical demand, but which are precisely realities we do not owe to ourselves.

At this point Kemp also raises objections against my assertion that we give our immediate love our own self's selfish form. He concedes that individuals do not know from their own experience that love can be unselfish (as that realization is precluded by love's self-forgetful nature), but they know it from the love with which they are met by other people.

Strictly speaking, the individual knows nothing about what elements of selfishness or unselfishness might be embodied in the other's love, but it is true that oftentimes we do not meet selfishness. Kemp has his sights set on something correct, which, however, I interpret in a different way. We are acutely aware of the amount of life-destruction to which our self-centeredness, and its reaction to other people's self-centeredness, gives rise. But for once we might marvel at how difficult it is for our self-centeredness to spoil our being together. How can this be? What makes it possible is this: what we meet in each other is so often first and foremost nature, understood as the realities for which we do not have ourselves to thank, but which are given to us. It is thanks to these realities that we make it through our lives together so surprisingly unscathed, keeping in mind how selfish we are.

8. The critical function of the gospel

Before I begin to deal with Professor Wingren's criticism, it may be relevant to call attention to the points on which we agree. He, too, refuses to believe that revelation is a precondition for hearing the ethical demand. Wingren speaks of the universal law that comes before and is independent of the preaching of the gospel. God's requirement that a person should willingly receive everything from God and willingly give it all away to their neighbor, is already put forward anonymously in creation, independently of the Scripture. The Christian proclamation merely articulates the requirement. Similarly, God's proper work (his *opus proprium*), which is to give, and which appears most clearly in the gospel, is already effective in creation, expressing itself in the elemental fact that we exist. "When the Bible speaks of God, it does not speak of something that human beings are supposed to meet and learn about in a specific religious act, in the same way as they learn about other objects in other acts. Rather, God is the creator, whose relation to human beings is given in the simple fact that they exist" (*Skapelsen och Lagen Creation and the Law* [Lund, 1958], 32, 39–40, 194; hereafter *SL*). Inasmuch as the demand is universal, it also belongs to philosophy. At one point, Wingren characterizes my method as a combination of philosophy and law, stating that he has nothing against that combination. "Between law and reason there is no hiatus: in that respect the philosophical framework and the theological content ought to be able to fit together seamlessly" (*Evangeliet och Kyrkan* [*The Gospel and the Church*] [Lund, 1960], 109; hereafter *EK*).

The ordinances under which we live must be pliable if they are to be of any benefit. "There is no such thing as a system of norms exempt from the criticism that is based on the requirement of love of one's neighbor" (*SL*, 158, 131). What Wingren opposes is, among other things, the so-called theology of ordinances, which encloses the natural law (the ethical demand) within certain ordinances—most notably, the people and the state—instead of letting the natural law (the ethical demand) be effective in the constantly changing relation to our neighbor. In that connection, Wingren characterizes my approach as the opposite of a theology of ordinances: "Beginning in the very relation to one's neighbor and not in the ordinance is, however, typical of Løgstrup" (*EK*, 195).

Wingren and I also agree polemically. I fully concur with his assertion that "Evangelical Christianity's relatively poorly balanced stance on the surrounding cultural life in modern times is connected with the fact that the doctrine of the law has been sorely neglected, for only on the level of the law is it possible to take a balanced view of contemporary culture . . ." (*SL*, 184).

Wingren's view is, then, that although the law is operative independently of the gospel, it will not do to portray its operation independently of the gospel. He therefore levels the following criticism at my account: that the critical function of the gospel is absent from it. Since I have accounted for the critical function of the radical demand in the individual's conscience and in respect of the social norms, however, the question is how the gospel's critical function differs from that of the radical demand.

Wingren claims that the norms and institutions can only be criticized in the light of the gospel. This claim can be understood in one of two ways: either in general terms, or in terms of the history of theology. Let us consider these two possibilities separately.

If the claim is to be understood in general terms it is clearly wrong, as throughout the centuries the Christians have not had a monopoly on criticizing the social norms. It has been known to happen that while the people of the church waited until the battle between the church and the tyrants broke out, those in anticlerical and antireligious circles had already begun to fight when people's freedom and secular institutions such as democracy and parents' right to raise their own children were at stake. At any rate, it has not always been churchgoers alone who, conscious of their responsibility, have battled social norms and conventions that oppressed people, robbed them of their freedom, and destroyed their institutions. Often those who fought were people who would not pay heed to any message of the death and resurrection of Christ. Naturally Wingren knows this as well as anyone. But what, then, is his intention?

He wishes to make it clear that there "exists no radical demand apart from the preaching of Christ's death" (*SL*, 204). In response to this, it must first be said that Jesus' intensification of the Old Testament law in his Sermon on the Mount is not a proclamation of the importance of his own death on the cross. Nor indeed can Wingren believe that it is, given that he can say that there is no contradiction between the natural commandment and Jesus Christ's intensification of it. But apart from that, what Wingren means to say is that the law has another function, a "blind" and "useless" one, as he expresses it, other than merely moving one to actions performed for the benefit of one's neighbor and for the neighbor's sake. The law points beyond itself, existing for the sake of a kingdom other than its own. And this other function is to demonstrate that it does not succeed in making a person's will conform to God's will. That means leaving a person with no way out. No person can ever, of his or her own free will, conform to God's will, and therefore each person must die. One could therefore also say that the decisive function of the law is the death of the individual person, who cannot enter the kingdom of God without it. Therefore the one human life that conformed to God's will—namely, Christ's human life—did not conform due to the law, but due to his living in another kingdom than the kingdom of the law: the kingdom of God that he himself proclaimed. And that is why it takes the account of Christ's life to expose the complete function of the law, the real radicality of the demand (*SL*, 209–211).

So Wingren understands the ethical demand (the law) in such a way that only through the congregation's proclamation of the works of Christ can we come to realize the implications of the demand in its radicality. However, this much is certain, whether one wishes to understand the radicality in this way or not: such an understanding is not necessary to subject the ordinances of social life to a decisive and thorough criticism. The ethical demand does not necessarily have to gain its content from a theological presentation of Christ's life and works in order to bring about a devastating criticism of customary norms and institutions. It is important to maintain this point, for otherwise we are guilty of creating an illusory barrier between Christians and non-Christians.

But next we must ask: Wherein should the gospel's criticism of the social norms consist, if it is to be different from the criticism exercised by the ethical demand? I am unable to see any difference, and I cannot see that there can be any. If there is a criticism that cannot be exercised according to the content of the ethical demand, but only in the name of the gospel, then there must be social norms that only concern those who believe the gospel but do not concern those who do not believe the gospel. In that case, an applied Christian ethic does exist. But does Wingren believe this?

Wingren is right on another point, though, which is that the activity of the ethical demand in our conscience gains a significance in the light of the gospel that it does not have without the gospel: pointing towards another kingdom than the kingdom of the law. But that is something different from exercising a criticism of the social norms that is not already exercised by the ethical demand. This means that the gospel supplies those who believe it with a further incentive to exercise the same substantive criticism with respect to morality, rights, conventions, and institutions as do those who do not believe the gospel are capable of exercising, prompted by the ethical demand. In my understanding of the question, however, the gospel does not give the Christian an opportunity to exercise a new and different kind of substantive criticism of the social norms.

What Wingren finds lacking in me is my failure to account for the gospel giving the individual sovereignty and freedom towards the naturally given forms of life that are, at the same time, confirmed and transformed (*EK*, 180). Then again, I suppose Wingren does not mean that the gospel supplies a particularly Christian reason for the transformation of the forms of life. If Wingren does not mean this, then we agree—and would that not mean his polemic really amounts to no more than establishing that I am treating a different problem than the one he is treating?

Two questions must be kept separate: (1) Does faith have any consequences for ethics? The answer to that must be "yes." I have expressed this by saying that faith gives us a new motivation to do the works that are demanded in our relationship with our neighbor. (2) Is faith's critical function in respect of the social norms substantively different from the ethical demand's? I believe the answer to this must be "no." As far as I can assess, Wingren has not kept these two questions separate in his polemic.

What Wingren would have said was that the gospel puts the death of the human being in a new light. Death is not understood biologically. That, however, has nothing to do with criticism of the social norms.

However, as mentioned earlier, Wingren's claim that the social norms can only be subject to criticism in the light of the gospel can also be understood in terms of the history of theology. In that case he is pointing out an error that the theologians necessarily commit: if they do not regard the actual demands addressed to us in the light of the gospel, they perceive the ordinances and their social norms statically. By way of example, Wingren refers to the German theologian Friedrich Gogarten, who in his work *Politische Ethik* distinguishes a radical, unconditional commandment (the "Thou-shalt" demand) from the moral conventions (the "One-does-this-or-that" demands). According to Gogarten, the radical, unconditional commandment does not possess any critical power in respect of the politically given requirements. Indeed, he actually rejects such a critical function.

Having established this point, Wingren immediately proceeds to identify the view expressed in my work with the view in *Politische Ethik*, and he does so in spite of the fact that every one of my considerations concerning the tension between the radical demand and the social norms is excluded from Gogarten's work in advance, as he considers the relationship between the radical demand and the social norms to be unproblematic. This springs from Gogarten's stripping the "Thou-shalt" demand of content and regarding the "One-does-this-or-that" demands as purely conventional and only relevant to actions in which people do not have to engage themselves, but can perform in obedience to the letter of the demands. I have explicitly polemicized against all of this (see, for instance, *The Ethical Demand* [Notre Dame, 1997], 53–63).[6]

Wingren mentions that my polemic, like Gogarten's, is directed towards the brand of Christian ethics that finds its norms in the Scripture instead of objectively dealing with the problems we face. It is true that I pursue this line of argument, but I have more than one line of argument, and, precisely in the chapter in question (chap. 3), one of my most important lines of argument goes against a theology that regards the relationship between the radical demand and the social norms as unproblematic.

Apart from that, Wingren does realize that I regard the relationship as full of tension, and he declares that he agrees with me, expressing himself as follows: "Love of one's neighbor cannot be bound by given social norms, for in that case . . . the works would be confined within group boundaries . . . The needs of our neighbor can require the performance of an action for the neighbor's sake that has never ever been performed before, and which cannot therefore be given in any common norm. Our neighbor is a factor that breaks through the accepted convention and law" (*SL*, 108). This is exactly what Gogarten lacked a feeling for, and that is exactly what I take exception to.

But how can Wingren in one place grant that in my work I do not subscribe to a static theology of ordinances because I regard the relationship between the social norms and the radical demand as full of tension, while in another place reproaching me for paving the way for a theology of ordinances because I do not allow the gospel to criticize the norms and institutions? What makes Wingren ignore the decisive contrast between Gogarten's view and mine? The answer is clear. Wingren is not interested in the question of the ethical demand's criticism of the social norms. He is concerned with another problem, namely, the gospel's criticism of the social norms. And since neither Gogarten nor I deal with the issue Wingren is dealing with, Wingren infers that Gogarten and I hold the same opinion.

9. Transcendental objections

The Danish pastor Rudolf Arendt (writing in the journal *Dansk teologisk Tidsskrift,* 1959, no. 2) has subjected *The Ethical Demand* to a criticism based on the philosophy that goes by the name of transcendental idealism—and Arendt particularly adheres to the form given to this philosophy by the Swedish theologian Anders Nygren. Allow me to give two examples of Arendt's mode of arguing.

The first example has to do with the concept of "a priori," which, whether in a formal or a material sense, is a concept that is foreign to my argumentation. It is, however, a basic concept in Arendt's transcendental philosophy and one that he must therefore force upon my investigation, proclaiming that trust—which I have expounded as giving rise to the demand—is an a priori. Arendt assumes without hesitation that when he regards trust as an a priori, I must naturally do the same, after which he sets about explaining Nygren's theory of the ethical a priori. He then goes on to raise the objection against me that I, along with Nygren and Arendt, certainly ought to know that an a priori can never be material but only formal. How, then, he suggests, could I ever conceive of making anything as material as trust into an a priori—as though I would ever have even dreamed of regarding trust as an a priori.

Moving on to the second example, I have dealt with the relationship between the radical ethical demand and social norms, using the metaphor that social norms are the prism through which the ethical demand is refracted. It is the ethical demand's functioning I had in mind, as I have indeed expressly stated. And it is evident from the context that my considerations concern the demand's functioning in the individual's ethical-existential decision. I use the prism metaphor to say that the individual's obedience towards the ethical demand is hidden, that it cannot be checked by outsiders, and that the individual cannot use it to justify his or her actions. I have furthermore said that social norms are sometimes guidelines indicating the action in which our obedience towards the ethical demand should find its form, that they are sometimes inadequate, and that they are sometimes misleading.

What does Arendt's rendition make of this? The rendition makes it into a claim on my part that there is no relationship between the ethical demand and social norms, that the ethical demand cannot affect the norms or transform them, that the norms are good and valid by virtue of their very existence, and that an ethical relation to them is out of the question.

What is the intention of such a misrepresentation? That question is not difficult to answer. The intention is to connect my exposition of the ethical demand with Nygren's ethical a priori, his basic formal ethical category. The fact of the matter is that, due to its formal nature, this basic ethical category is unable to affect social norms, and so I must have the view forced upon me that the ethical demand cannot affect the social norms either. If not, my exposition of the ethical demand cannot be connected with Nygren's formal ethical a priori, and Arendt would not have been able to present his argument for how much better it would have been if, instead of writing *The Ethical Demand,* I had written one of Nygren's books. The fact that Nygren's and my own lines of thinking have nothing to do with one another seems to be of little concern to Arendt.

To Arendt, my book is a somewhat coincidental opportunity to elaborate on Nygren's transcendental philosophy. What I say is interpreted not in terms of my assumptions, but in terms of Nygren's. My phenomenological analyses are therefore of little or no interest to Arendt as far as their content is concerned. His interest lies mainly in finding out where—if one corrected them a little—it would be possible to place these analyses in a transcendental system. The nature of the argument is therefore as follows: If we apply the distinctions of transcendental philosophy to my work, it turns out to contain serious ambiguities. Wherein do they consist? Why, they consist in a lack of compliance with the distinctions of transcendental philosophy. But the fact that Arendt is capable of using the distinctions of transcendental philosophy to demonstrate the ambiguities in my work— ambiguities that he has inserted by means of the very same distinctions— is hardly surprising. If a criticism is to be convincing, however, one must take a different approach. First, Arendt—without putting forward his own philosophical assumptions—would have had to show how, in my investigation, I was guilty of contradicting myself, ending up in cul-de-sacs, distorting facts, and so on. Arendt could *then* have moved on to demonstrate that I could have avoided all those things if I had held his sound philosophy. But this is precisely what Arendt has not done, but instead, honest man that he is, he has begun by drawing attention to the philosophy he assumes and which he intends to show is not present in my work— which is, of course, in his opinion a great deficiency in it. Arendt has used my book as a sort of drill ground on which he has practiced the motions and turns of transcendental philosophy. That is all very well for those who wish to practice such things, but, strictly speaking, it is no business of mine.

I incidentally consider it all but impossible that Nygren would agree with Arendt in the way he has used Nygren's philosophy.

I shall nevertheless respond to Arendt on two points. The first is what one might call the question of the superfluousness of the historically existing proclamation.

Arendt initially argues in purely epistemological terms. I have claimed that it is certainly conceivable that there are features of our existence of which we were unable to become aware until a proclamation of these features had become a historical fact, but that after the proclamation had shown us these features, we might be able to recognize them on our own without seeking refuge in the proclamation. Arendt protests against this with the following observation: If things stand as I say, then the proclamation must not only have shown us the features in question, but must "also have brought about a decisive change, a sort of mutation, in our cognitive apparatus, imbuing it with a new capacity it did not previously possess" (*Dansk teologisk Tidsskrift,* 1959, no. 2, p. 100). And since that can hardly be the case, Arendt concludes, the relevant feature of our existence cannot be understood without the proclamation. But on what kind of strange notion of our cognition is that argument based? Is our cognitive capacity considered here as an apparatus that has been constructed once and for all, and which at all times operates in the same fashion? That is a pure construct, which completely disregards the fact that man lives historically. True, there is in us an apparatus that does not change, namely our senses, but it is not by means of our senses that we understand a proclamation. We understand it by means of our historically defined existence, and that is certainly no apparatus.

But Arendt then goes on to present the more concrete claim that since I make the proclamation of Jesus superfluous and deny its revelational character, I am on the wrong track. Arendt is right in saying that—if we disregard the authority with which Jesus spoke—I do, in this respect, make his proclamation superfluous, but Arendt still owes me a proof that this puts me on the wrong track. It remains a claim. I will, however, explain myself in greater detail. In my estimation, those scholars of the New Testament who distinguish in the proclamation of Jesus between his ethical proclamation and his eschatological message concerning the coming and the appearance of the Kingdom of God are right. His ethical proclamation, which we know of, not least from the Sermon on the Mount (although there are also other portions of his proclamation, such as the story of the good Samaritan, that are independent of his eschatological message), consists in an intensification of the law of the Old Testament. His ethical proclamation is a statement of God's *universal* demand. It is as old as creation, it has always been there, although its radicality has been over-looked and was not heard until "now," in the proclamation of Jesus. But after it has been stated in the proclamation of Jesus, we also hear it with-out this proclamation.

The eschatological message of Jesus is a different story, however, for Jesus does not stop at proclaiming the coming of the Kingdom of God. Jesus also proclaims that this kingdom is already appearing, and doing so in his own proclamation of it and through his works, in his driving out of demons. Here, he himself is not superfluous. And this is one of the pre-conditions that enabled the congregation's faith in him and its proclamation of him to come into existence—although there is, incidentally, a dif-ference between his own understanding of being part of the eschatological turn that the coming Kingdom of God will bring, on the one hand, and the congregation's understanding that the eschatological turn has already arrived with him, on the other.

Thus, I believe that we cannot speak as summarily of the proclamation of Jesus as Arendt does, but that we must distinguish between the part of it in which Jesus renders himself superfluous and the part in which he does not.

Allow me to add, by the way, that the ethical proclamation of Jesus is not found in the scriptures of the New Testament attributed to John any more than it is found in Paul. Here it has not merely been rendered super-fluous but has disappeared. In John and Paul, the intensified demand is not God's universal law, but appears only with a Christological justifica-tion. This is understandable, because they were solely interested in pro-claiming Jesus as the one with whom the eschatological turn had already taken place. In addition, they were able to give (or to put it more correctly, they were unable to avoid giving) their proclamation a mythical form. Today we regard it as a deficiency that the proclamation of God's univer-sal law is not found in their proclamation, a deficiency that we must mend—also because we cannot think mythically, but are bound to replace the New Testament authors' mythical thinking with historical thinking. Assisting us in this correction is the knowledge we have of the proclama-tion of Jesus from the first three Gospels.

In this connection Arendt offers a rather odd methodological obser-vation. Whether the proclamation of Jesus is superfluous or not "must be decided *in advance,* before the investigation is initiated. The decision can never be made as a result at one stage or another of the investigation, as the entire course of the investigation and its results are determined by which of the two points of departure we choose." Who has decided this question in advance? Why, the philosophical system to which Arendt adheres. Arendt wishes to have the investigation's method fixed in advance. It is not to depend on the material. Arendt does not want to know what life is like, but he does want to keep his methods in order. But who says that life must illustrate the distinctions we have in advance? Might it not be conceivable that life was too unruly for that? How can we find out whether it is so? Precisely by means of a phenomenological description.

In the final analysis, the difference between Arendt and myself is a philosophical one. Allow me, therefore, by way of conclusion to say a few words about it. I can concentrate our disagreement on a single concept: I do not share Arendt's concept of validity.

Transcendental philosophy, Arendt says, does not deal with the content of cognition as such, but rather sees it as its task to get a grip on the tacit preconditions for our cognition, of which validity may be the most important. As an example, Arendt mentions the law of causality, which is not itself a statement of experience but the validity of which Kant held to be a tacit precondition for our statements of experience. Arendt goes on to say: "The validity of cognition is not itself part of the content of cognition, although it always concerns its content. The question of the validity of cognition lies outside the area in which the law of causality is valid." But there is something here that is not right. Because the terms "validity" and "to be valid" mean the same thing, Arendt claims with his second sentence that the question of the validity of cognition lies outside the area in which cognition has validity. This is an obvious self-contradiction. The reason it was possible for this to escape Arendt's attention was that he used the word in two different meanings: the meaning in everyday language, and the meaning in the type of philosophy to which he adheres. In everyday language, having validity and being valid means to have binding consequences for a certain area, for which reason it is meaningless to speak of, for instance, the validity of a certain cognition in abstraction from the area for which that cognition has validity. When Arendt nevertheless does so, it is because his philosophy attributes an entirely different meaning to the word "validity."

Let us look at the two meanings separately, beginning with the meaning in everyday language. As mentioned, "to have validity" means to have binding consequences for a certain area—and perhaps only for a certain period. Therefore one cannot say that something is valid, pure and simple; one must always bear in mind the area, and possibly the period, for which something has validity. But it is also possible to say something about what can have validity. What is required for something to have binding consequences? What is required is that it is formulated and fixed and can function as a yardstick. It is therefore desirable that the formulation should be detailed enough and the fixing precise enough to allow one to see which consequences are binding (Hans Lipps, *Untersuchungen zu einer hermeneutischen Logik* [Frankfurt a. M., 1938], 17).

And now to the philosophical meaning. This meaning arises in the following way: instead of allowing the validity to mean the binding consequences that a formulation or fixing has by virtue of functioning as a yardstick in a certain field, the validity is made to rest in the formulation or fixing as such. The validity must rest in the judgement and its cognition as merely true. But then, what does the validity add? The answer is: ideality. This actually means, however, that the meaning transcendental philosophy attributes to validity arises as a result of emptying validity of any content, going on to let its emptiness bear witness to valid cognition's ideality. To put it differently: because validity is allowed to rest in the judgment dissociated from the area for which the judgment is binding, validity is also dissociated from this area, after which one takes its dis-sociatedness, its ab-soluteness, to be identical with ideality.

10. Two peculiar arguments

A number of people have raised objections to the connection I made between gift and indebtedness. For instance: "If one has received a gift, then one owes nothing," as Professor Lomholt puts it. "Nothing" indeed! Lomholt must, throughout his life, have been spared from ever receiving as a gift anything that was meant to stand, hang, or lie in full view since he knows nothing of the conflicts to which that can give rise. It is correct that when one receives a gift, one does not owe the other person anything in return, and in that sense, Lomholt is right in saying that "gift and debt do not rhyme well." It is quite a different matter, however, that one most certainly does owe the other person the consideration of treating the gift as a gift—say, not packing it away if its function is, in fact, to stand, hang, or lie in full view.

And now to the second peculiar argument, which I shall put succinctly: I have claimed that the ethical demand (in its capacity as radical) is silent. And since a Christian political party as such believes it is able to speak in the name of the ethical and radical demand, anyone who accepts that the ethical demand is silent cannot join a Christian political party. Here Stangerup objects that this makes me the one to break the silence of the ethical demand, since in its name I say "you cannot be a member of a Christian political party."

Quite bluntly, in my view that is sophistry. Let us nevertheless take a closer look at the logical structure of the argument. From a formal point of view, what I say against the members of a Christian political party is: "It is wrong of you to claim the demand is not silent." That is all I say, but in Stangerup's opinion I cannot do so without becoming guilty of a self-contradiction, since by doing so, I myself also break the silence of the ethical demand. However, my view that it is wrong to claim the demand is not silent is nothing more than the negative version of what I say positively: it is right to claim the demand is silent. If, therefore, I cannot say without contradicting myself that it is wrong the demand is not silent, then likewise I cannot say without contradicting myself that it is right the demand is silent. Stangerup's argument therefore actually amounts to saying that I, with my claim that the demand is silent, am breaking its silence. But that argument is a paradox. Why? Well, if the demand is silent, the sentence "the demand is silent" is false, since with that sentence I break the silence of the demand. If I am right in saying the demand is silent, the Christian political party is right in saying the demand is not silent. On the other hand, if the demand is not silent, then my claim that "the demand is silent" may be true, since by making that claim I break the silence of the demand. If the Christian political party is right in saying the demand is not silent, I may be right in saying the demand is silent. In other words: when the sentence is false, it is true, and when it is true, it may be false. Or: although the claim of the Christian political party and my claim contradict one another, we may both be right. The logical structure of the argument Stangerup employs is that of the paradox, which naturally makes the argument useless. And although Stangerup has not clarified for himself the logical structure of the argument, I still find it puzzling that he did not sense that he was getting himself into some sort of sophistry.

Allow me to add that this paradox is of the same type as Epimenides' paradox, and that there are quite a number of them. Logicians have shown the keenest interest in this sort of paradox, the problem being to determine how they might be avoided. So if Stangerup will not allow himself to be convinced by me, I can recommend that he test his line of argument strictly logically, using, for instance, the elucidations offered in Tarski's famous treatise *The Semantic Conception of Truth*. He can familiarize himself with these problems in Professor Hartnack's *Filosofiske Essays* (Philosophical Essays) (Copenhagen, 1957), 112–125, as well as his *Filosofiske problemer* (Philosophical Problems and Argumentations) (Copenhagen, 1958), chapter 5.B.4.

Notes

1. Translators' note: By "human" Løgstrup means in this context "that which belongs to, or is accessible to, humans as humans, apart from Christian belief." Because Løgstrup regards the ethical demand as human in this sense, he can develop his ethics as a philosophical ethics.

2. Translators' note: Løgstrup refers to the chapter "Det etiske valg" in *Kunst og etik*.

3. Translators' note: This and the following quotation are from Løgstrup, *The Ethical Demand* (Notre Dame: University of Notre Dame Press, 1997), 122.

4. Translators' note: The Criminal Law Amendment Act of 1 June 1945 regulated the persecution of Danes collaborating with the German occupying forces during the Second World War. H. Østergaard-Nielsen criticized this law for including collaboration before 29 August 1943, during which period the Danish goverment conducted a policy of active collaboration with the Germans. Collaboration before that date, he believed, ought to be regarded as morally reprehensible but not as a criminal offence, because it was in agreement with the official Danish policy prior to that date.

5. Translators' note: For "the ultimate authority," cf. Løgstrup, *The Ethical Demand*, 171.

6. Translators' note: In the Danish original Løgstrup only refers to a page (corresponding to 55–56) where he acknowledges the possibility of external compliance with the social norms. He does not refer to the wider context that points to the limits of this possibility. To avoid misunderstandings, the reference has been extended to include the whole context.

TWO

The Sovereign
Expressions of Life

In *Opgør med Kierkegaard* (Controverting Kierkegaard), Løgstrup's critical assessment of Kierkegaard's understanding of Christian belief provides the context for his exposition of the notion of the sovereign expressions of life. These are formulated and elucidated in Part Three, which carries the title "The movement of infinity." The allusion is to Kierkegaard's notion of "the infinite movement of resignation," which consists in the individual's renouncing everything to which he or she is attached in this world for the sake of loving God alone. For Kierkegaard, this movement preconditions another, the movement of faith, the making of which restores the person to life in the world.

Løgstrup sets the scene for his account of the sovereign expressions of life by comparing "Sartre's and Kierkegaard's respective characterizations of demonic self-enclosedness" (Part Three, chapter IV). For this, he introduces into the discussion Sartre's *Le diable et le bon dieu* (*The Devil and the Good Lord*), a play set in sixteenth-century Germany at the time of the peasant revolt. The main protagonist is Goetz, an army commander responsible for besieging the city of Worms, which was in revolt. Born out of wedlock, Sartre's Goetz is despised by the world. He sets about revenging himself on both world and God by seeking to epitomize absolute evil. Heinrich, a priest from Worms, betrays his city to Goetz in order to save his fellow priests from execution by the people. However, when Heinrich declares that no human being is capable of achieving the good, Goetz takes this as a challenge and, steering now towards the opposite extreme, determines to become a saint.

On Løgstrup's reading of the play, Sartre's Goetz, in dedicating himself to evil, performs a movement of infinity, but of a demonic kind. For in it "he shrinks into himself in a wickedness that is infinite" (*Opgør med Kierkegaard* [Copenhagen, 1968], 88). According to Løgstrup, the very notion of such a movement draws its substance from Kierkegaard's idea that, ultimately, all human existence consists in a relationship to eternity. Consequently, eternity "marks, indeed, determines all of human existence, even when the individual is unaware of it or does not want to recognize it" (ibid., 91).

From the analysis of Sartre's Goetz it is but a short step to a comparison of that character with the eponymous figure in Goethe's play *Goetz von Berlichingen*. Despite sharing a common protagonist, Goethe's and Sartre's plays are, Løgstrup insists, completely different. Most notably, whereas Sartre's characters are driven by their ideas, the actions of Goethe's personae are the manifestations of character. In contrast to Goetz von Berlichingen, who is trusting and whose word is his bond, Adelbert von Weislingen, his adversary, is vain, faithless, and a philanderer. Weislingen betrays Goetz by succumbing to erotic allure and flattery. In the extract that follows, Løgstrup uses Goetz's conduct towards Weislingen to illustrate two sovereign expressions of life, trust and openness.

Having provided brief accounts of the two thematically linked plays and illustrated Kierkegaard's idea of the movement of infinity by reference to Sartre's Goetz in sections a–c of chapter IV, Løgstrup takes up the theme of the sovereign expressions of life in section d of that chapter. To facilitate comparison with the Danish text, the original chapter numbers and section lettering have been retained.

IVd. The sovereign expressions of life

Kierkegaard and Sartre neglect a large part of human life. What that part comprises can best be brought out by means of a distinction between two kinds of phenomenon, which, for brevity, I shall call "the obsessive" and "the sovereign." Let me offer three examples of "obsessive" or "encircling" phenomena: offence, jealousy, and envy.

In taking offence, one makes oneself the victim of an affront, notwithstanding that one knows in one's heart of hearts that there is no reason to feel aggrieved. Even when it is not pure invention, the affront will have been occasioned by some trifle of which one makes too much. There is no proportionality between what occasioned the affront and one's reaction to it, and in that resides the ludicrousness and pettiness characteristic of offence. Often, offence's preoccupation with some imaginary or trivial affront serves to save one from having to face up to one's own fault, even when the latter is not so grave as to make acknowledgment of it a great matter. But perhaps the individual in question has too high an opinion of himself to be able to bear the thought of having acted wrongly, and so offence serves to deflect attention from his own misdemeanor, and this it achieves by making him the wronged party.

An individual is seized by jealousy when another displaces him or threatens to do so in respect of a relationship with a third party, which relationship the former believes to be rightfully his. He finds himself ousted from his place in the affections of the one he loves, be it an object of romantic love or a friend. He assumes that he is entitled to be the preferred choice, inasmuch as the relationship is deemed exclusive. So he is cheated of what is his by right. His bitterness is directed not so much at his rival— who is the object of envy, rather—as towards the one whose favor he covets and who does wrong in bestowing it upon the rival.

It is not, however, the case that the richer the relationship from which the jealousy-stricken individual is ousted, the greater his or her jealousy. The peculiar thing is that these two features need bear no relation to each other: on the contrary, the most glaring disparity may obtain. That a given relationship is unworthy of jealousy does not render the jealousy any less extreme, with all other and far more valuable relations being held of no account, indeed, being forfeited for the sake of this one paltry relationship. Life-enhancing opportunities are far from always the object of the struggle: as often as not, jealousy is a mania engendered by weakness.

In contradistinction to envy, where only two parties are involved, jealousy is a trilateral relationship. In the former case, the one begrudges the other his or her abilities, qualities, position, assets, lot in life, or whatever it may be. But envy does not merely spring from the other's having what one lacks oneself, for that circumstance might equally well elicit admiration. What is required is that the things one has to do without are of such a nature that one feels unable to come to terms with the lack thereof. And one regards the other's possession of them as illicit. Properly considered, he is not worthy of it. The enviable person's advantages are undeserved and the envious individual feels deprived of his due.

What jealousy and envy have in common is that they both spring from powerlessness. For after all, the jealous individual can do nothing to become the favorite and win the good graces that he covets. Nor can the envious individual alter the distribution of advantages and disadvantages. In their powerlessness, both the jealous and the envious are thrust back upon themselves, immersing themselves in their own exclusion. They bury themselves in their rancor and take a certain relish in doing so. Jealousy and envy are encircling thoughts and emotions in which the individual imprisons himself.

All movements of thought and feeling that pursue their own obsessive course—such as, for instance, hatred and the desire for vengeance—are self-supporting, with most of the grievances that sustain them being ones they themselves engender. Excessive distrust leads to putting the worst construction on everything. Taking satisfaction in the conception of oneself as the wronged party, one has to invent wrongs with which to feed it. It is hardly accurate to call what the individual encloses himself with "emotions": they are rather fixations, whose paltry emotionality consists in the self's forcing them to revolve around him. Attached to his leash and urged on by his whip, these thoughts go round and round in the self's own private ring.

The contraries of the obsessive movements of self-enclosedness are the sovereign expressions of life: trust and mercy, for example. Unlike pity, which cannot be called sovereign, if only for the reason that often there is nothing to be done—the sufferer's situation being irremediable—mercy, qua expression of the will to transform the situation of the person in need, is sovereign. While pity is concern, perhaps resigned concern, and its object the person who has been disadvantaged in life, mercy draws its impetus from the thought that the other has received his or her life in order to realize it and is now hampered in so doing.

The sovereign expression of life draws its content from the specific situation and the relation to the other, which is to say, from my conception of that situation and relation, of their actual circumstances and history.

The expression of life is not something to be applied. Principles, precepts, and maxims are applied. The expression of life cannot be applied, but can only be realized, as I realize myself in it. This is due to its sovereign character. It does not rigidify the situation but frees it up, transforms it, which is why the individual must involve himself in it throughout.

All of this stands in contrast to the obsessive and encircling movements of thought and feeling. Once a person is under their sway, agency is driven by contingencies. Action is reactive, not sovereign. The individual is simply a function of the situation, whereas in what concerns the sovereign expression of life the situation is a function of the agent: we turn the situation round through trust, through mercy, through the openness of speech.

But is not Sartre's Goetz as sovereign as anyone? No, only in an external, arbitrary, and ruthless sense, and his arbitrariness and ruthlessness show his sovereignty to be a sham, an epiphenomenon arising from the compulsive course his thoughts and feelings have traced in seeking revenge for his fundamental defect.

Yet another difference between the sovereign expressions of life and the obsessive movements of thought and feeling is this: should battle be joined between them, between, say, sincerity and betrayal, there is no foregone conclusion that the sovereign expression of life will prevail. Far from it. But sovereignty has such weight that fear informs the opponent's countermeasures. To hold his own, he must find ways of subduing his fear of sincerity. However robust his public standing, fear will not elude him. Irrespective of who triumphs or who suffers defeat, in one respect it is an unequal game. The one party trusts to the sovereign expression of life and is able to do so because of the latter's sovereignty. The other party must resort to stratagems, tricks, and threats, since in the end his fight is a defensive one, even when ending in triumph.

Kierkegaard never spared the sovereign expressions of life so much as a thought. And that is no accident. He is forced to leave them out of account in order to preserve the role of self-reflection. For to say that the expressions of life are sovereign is to say that in them, the human person is—ipso facto—himself. He no longer has to reflect upon becoming an independent person, nor has he to reflect upon the task of becoming his true self; he has only to realize himself in the sovereign expression of life, and it is that expression of life—rather than reflection—that takes care of the person's selfhood. Kierkegaard is mistaken in thinking that only through religious reflection can the human person accomplish the task of becoming a self, as though we were not equipped with the sovereign expressions of life that accomplish it for us.

As we have seen, Kierkegaard operates with both a concrete and an abstract self. But Kierkegaard understands the human person's concretion only through what is individual: abilities, aptitudes, circumstances of life—in short, the individual in all that distinguishes him or her.

Kierkegaard leaves out the sovereign expressions of life. And since the self can only be won in relation to eternity, he conceives the person's true self as an abstract entity—as though it were not the case that a person becomes his true self, and concretely so, by realizing himself in the sovereign expressions of life and identifying himself with them.

But what has become, then, of the sovereign expressions of life? If they are absent in Kierkegaard, something must have taken their place! Their place must be occupied by something else! And so it is—by philistinism. The sovereign expressions of life are engulfed by conformity, are drowned in a life where the one individual imitates the other. For Kierkegaard, the universal disjunction is either to live in relation to the infinite idea or to live a life of conformism. The requirements enjoined upon us are either those of eternity or those of conformity. These alternatives recur in Heidegger with the difference there that eternity is replaced by death. But this disjunction is spurious. The sovereign expression of life also has a claim on us, and has it in virtue of being definitive; it is not first engendered by us through the deployment of vague mental powers. The expression of life, whether it takes the form of speech, action, or conduct, or all of these at once, is transmutable in a trice, quick as lightning: its fluidity, mutability, is eminent and yet it is definitive at every moment. It is no less definitive for being spontaneous: spontaneity does not figure in human existence as an indeterminate surge of life. In the most elemental manner conceivable, claims are imposed on human beings: they are implicit already in the definitiveness of the sovereign expression of life. A claim has entered into the spontaneous expression of life and has given it character, making it the definitive thing it is. And the claim is strong because it is so elemental. Let me offer an illustration. Let us imagine that we stand facing a destroyer who is trying to win us for his cause, but we know that he will shun no means in doing so and that he is not to be trusted. Face to face with the destroyer, we discover how much effort it takes to remain on our guard. The thought that, by talking things out, we would be able to dissuade the destroyer from his destructive enterprise keeps presenting itself; there is no eradicating it once and for all. We must keep telling ourselves that it is an illusion to think that we could talk things out, and must continually bear in mind that anything we say will be used to put a third vulnerable party out of the way. But why is that thought so persistent? Why do we need to make such an effort to restrain ourselves, and why do we experience doing so as nothing less than contrary to nature? It is because we are opposing the requirement inherent in speech that speech be open. To speak is to speak openly. The requirement comes from speech, springs from speech itself, is identical with its definitive character qua spontaneous expression of life, and is imposed by speech at the very instant in which I have recourse to it and realize myself in it. For all their spontaneity, the expressions of life are always, and antecedently, definitive. To realize oneself in them is thus to conform to the requirement that they be realized on their own definitive terms. The expression of life is indeed mine, but not in the sense that I invest it with its definitive character. My speech is indeed mine, and it is indeed up to me whether I will be open in my speech, but it is not I who have brought it about that the definitive feature of speech is its openness. If I deceive another or raise my guard, I challenge the definitive feature of speech which attaches to it in advance of, and independently of, me.

In order further to clarify the alternative to Kierkegaard's view, let me elaborate the relationship between Goetz von Berlichingen and Weislingen as it is presented to us at the beginning of Goethe's drama. Knowing that Goetz can deliver on both counts, Weislingen seeks information and advice from Goetz von Berlichingen, confident that Goetz will assist him to the best of his ability.

Now in the event, Goetz von Berlichingen does not deceive Weislingen. This is not because Goetz von Berlichingen is unaware that whenever he finds it expedient, Weislingen will misuse whatever Goetz offers him by way of support in word or action. Goetz von Berlichingen may also retain a vivid recollection of the many occasions on which Weislingen deceived him—and yet notwithstanding this, he does not take advantage of Weislingen's present difficulty to procure sweet revenge by giving Weislingen a taste of his own medicine. But why does Goetz von Berlichingen not do precisely that? We say that it is against his nature to do so, he cannot bring himself to act in that way, he is not sufficiently without substance to do so. But then how does a person acquire substance? He does so by identifying himself with the definitiveness inherent in the expressions of life through which he realizes his life. Through his identification with the definitiveness inherent in a complex of expressions of life, the individual becomes a concrete self. Goetz von Berlichingen may toy with the idea of exploiting the precarious situation in which Weislingen finds himself to lead him astray, bring about his downfall, and by so doing get him back for his past misdeeds—but never gets beyond merely toying with it.

What, then, have Kierkegaard and the existentialist to say about a character like Goethe's Goetz and his decisions? One or other of two things! Either: In the circles in which Goetz von Berlichingen grew up, it was good form to be honest and forthright. So he follows convention, conducts himself as the others do. He has yielded up his identity to the others, is not a self, not spirit.

Or else: In Weislingen's request for information and advice, Goetz von Berlichingen finds himself challenged, which is to say challenged by eternity, which is in turn to say removed from the great mass of people, from convention, set apart as a particular individual and rendered a self. Eternity challenges Goetz von Berlichingen in order to constitute him as an eternal self in obedience to the eternal demand. Eternity places Goetz von Berlichingen before the choice between obedience and disobedience and constitutes him as choice's abstract and empty subject.

Crucial to the understanding of both Kierkegaard and the existentialist is the fact that for them there is no concrete command which runs: Irrespective of your experience of the other as a traitor, you are to show him trust and offer him the assistance you think he needs (not necessarily the trust and the assistance he desires). What those words express is merely a convention, compliance with which does not render one a self. But what is there, then, for the existentialist theologian and philosopher? Only the empty demand to the effect that you live your life as demanded—and from which it follows what, in the particular concrete situation, you are to do. If Goetz von Berlichingen yields to his thirst for revenge he fails to live as demanded, and ergo, he should not yield to it. As if he did not already know from his thirst for revenge that it is evil. If Goetz von Berlichingen shows Weislingen trust and offers him his help, then Goetz lives as demanded, and ergo, he ought to show trust and offer his help. As if he did not already know from the nature of trust and help that they are possibilities given him so that he may realize them.

But if it is the case that Goetz von Berlichingen, as portrayed by Goethe, has become so concrete and substantial through his identification with the definitive in the expressions of life of trust and speech that he neither dissembles nor wreaks revenge, what then? Well, then he is not sufficiently abstract and devoid of substance for it to be a question of choice and decision. But what explanation of his conduct are Kierkegaard and the existentialist able to offer? None other than that which says that he conducts himself in conformity with convention—he does as others do.

But it is not that simple. There is a difference between whether Goetz von Berlichingen is open and trusting because it is for that that his life has been given him, or whether he does so because that is what custom requires. If he acts out of conformity, he will scarcely be able to avoid acting ineptly. He will not find in what is merely custom and convention the impulses to take the specific circumstances informing his relationship to Weislingen into account. If he is simply anxious to satisfy the common standards of chivalry, to adhere to that code, he would walk, eyes closed, straight into Weislingen's trap. Good form prompts him merely to follow his nose. His conformity would turn his trust into credulity, his openness into indiscretion.

If, instead, he is anxious to help Weislingen and show him trust, he will conduct himself otherwise. He will neither trivialize nor disguise the fact, neither from Weislingen nor from himself, that it is a traitor he is dealing with. He will discover Weislingen's traps, thwart him whenever he is able, and take all precautionary measures. He will take up the challenge, acting prudently and shrewdly, narrowing the scope for Weislingen's treachery as far as he can. He will let Weislingen know that he is aware of what he can expect from him. Yet in all of this, he will still be giving him a chance—the chance which consists in his not washing his hands of him;

and in so doing Goetz von Berlichingen will realize trust and openness—on his own terms and not on Weislingen's treacherous terms. The opportunity he offers Weislingen is that of being won over to his side against his own treacherous self. No matter how convinced Goetz von Berlichingen may be that this opportunity, too, Weislingen will abuse—he is to have it all the same. But he cherishes no illusions: at the same time, he does everything in his power to neutralize Weislingen's schemes. Were Goetz von Berlichingen, by contrast, merely conformist, demonstratively credulous, and indiscreet, he would be inviting Weislingen to dupe him, thereby further entrenching him in his ways. Only by unsparingly letting Weislingen know what he thinks of him—without breaking with him—does he give him a chance. Conformity rigidifies the expressions of life—they become templates, poses, gestures. If, instead, they are realized, since it is for that end that each has received his life, it lies with the individual to let the definitive expression of life thrust its way through in even the most complicated and unpropitious of situations.

I mentioned earlier that, for Kierkegaard, only what is eternally certain is certain: unless God binds him, the individual is unbound, left to his own experimentation with himself. But no such phenomenon exists, I would contend. For experimentation with oneself to be possible, the sovereign expressions of life would have to be indifferent. But indifferent is what they are not; they are definitive. Alternatively, their definitiveness notwithstanding, the sovereign expressions of life would have to be neutralizable. But they are not neutralizable either, since it is in virtue of their definitiveness that they make claims on us. It might be said of an actor that in playing a part he or she experiments with another persona. But this renders the sovereign expressions of life neither indifferent nor neutral. On the contrary, the actor shows just how definitive and demanding the sovereign expressions of life are in the life of the character whom he plays, whether that character realizes himself through them or betrays and misuses them. If, by contrast, a person seeks to be an actor playing himself, he fancies that he can play around with and do as it suits him with the sovereign expressions of life, as though they were neither definitive nor demanding. But in that case, he is under a misapprehension: the sovereign expressions of life are the stronger, rendering the person who seeks to experiment on himself a poseur or a liar. The person portrayed by Kierke-gaard says: When I speak or act I experiment with my speech or agency, I am not inside my words or action, I am always outside of them. But that is impossible: one of two things results. Either he will speak and act as the poseur that he is. The non-natural has become his second nature, and he is in the grip of a fantasy if he believes that because he puts on an act, he stands outside his words and gestures—as though his affectation were mere play-acting, while he, intact, which is to say, unaffected, is able to re-main outside it. He is steeped in his affectation, not merely in some exter-nal sense, but as the self that he is. Or, alternatively, the person patently does indeed stand outside his words or actions, like the liar, hypocrite, and cheat who pretends that his words or actions are true, sincere, and honest. The experimental stance vis-à-vis oneself is either a theory that the poseur uses to flatter himself—there is more to him than affectation—or else it is a theory that may be used to trivialize and render innocuous lying, hypoc-risy, and deception. In the full knowledge that what he passes off as true, sincere, and honest is mendacious, hypocritical, and deceitful, he pretends to himself that in virtue of his possession of such knowledge he is not a liar, a hypocrite, and a fraud

Neglect of the sovereign and definitive expressions of life leads to two things: notions of choice, determination, and freedom become abstrac-tions, and the choice between existing as an individual in relation to the infinite idea or living a life of conformity takes center stage, and we are left with existentialism's vacuous talk of the vacuous self.

Kierkegaard's capital error, which the existentialists, both philosophi-cal and theological, have perpetuated, is that he, and they with him, make the individual's choice, decision, and freedom alone that which renders life definitive—as though our existence were not already and antecedently something definitive in each of its, as it were, anonymous expressions of life. That which is alone subject to the individual's choice, determination, and freedom is whether to fulfill the definitiveness which, already and an-tecedently, attaches to the sovereign expression of life through which the individual realizes himself—or to be guilty of its dereliction.

Let me in conclusion illustrate the problem by reference to another of Sartre's plays, by turning to Johanna and Werner's relationship in *Les séquestrés d'Altona* (*The Condemned of Altona*). Werner is a Hamburg law-yer living happily married to Johanna, when his father, who has been told by doctors that he has not long to live, requires of Werner that he replace him in his post as head of Germany's largest shipyard and fleet, a mighty concentration of financial power. The older brother Franz, for whom this position was intended, has, for reasons I shall not enter into but which in fact furnish the play with its central theme, disqualified himself for the post. Johanna, knowing that it will be a disaster for Werner and herself if he yields to his father's demand, does what she can to prevent it, but in vain. As soon as he is within the familial environment, everything Werner says or does is a reflection of the jealousy engendered in childhood by his father's slighting of him in favor of Franz. In one scene, Werner appears to be standing out against his father, but Johanna intervenes and interrupts him: "You're listening to yourself speak. Once you get mired in self-pity we are lost . . . Just say no, without shouting and without laughing." Johanna senses that neither sentiment nor self-pity is able to invest a decision with substance. But what, then, is required? My answer is that what is required is that the person identifies himself with a sovereign and definitive expression of life. What this consists of, in Werner's case, is simple: it is his love for Johanna. Were Werner capable of identifying with that, he would be capable of giving substance to a decision that ran counter to his father's wishes. But more powerful than Werner's love for Johanna and hers for him is his jealousy, and so he gives in to it.

But what is Kierkegaard's position on this? He maintains that eternity alone is able to invest a decision with permanence; only eternity can put an end to the shrinking into oneself. The possibility of a cure consists in the help that resides in the absurdity that for God all things are possible. But the difficulty of accepting such assistance is the greatest thinkable, Kierkegaard adds, and is so because the person in need is allowed no say in how he is to be helped; he must leave it all to God, and unconditionally to boot. To be helped he must surrender his self and become as nothing in the hand of the succorer. And that is the last thing he wants. There is nothing the self recoils from more; rather be the self that one is and suffer the torments of the damned than seek help.

But this means that the difficulty of accepting religious help is one Kierkegaard has rendered so acute that the needy individual is driven to cling to his distress. The religious remedy as a possible cure is rendered so impossible that it can only serve as an incentive to ever more intensified self-enclosedness. This is the result of making the relation to God abstract, of abstracting from all the opportunities for cure that life presents in the way of opportunities—in the individual's relation to his work, to other people, to the world around him—for spontaneous flourishing. These lie outside Kierkegaard's range of vision because our ordinary, temporal, earthly life has nothing to do with eternity. It is a life that exists merely to be sacrificed, not to be lived.

V. Absolute good

I return to *Le diable et le bon dieu* to proceed with its second half. If disasters had struck the powerless and poor when Goetz waged war on them, they rain down on them with a vengeance now that he has started to love them. The catalogue of sufferings to which his love subjects them is nothing if not comprehensive. His estates and his castle, all that he owns, he gives to the poor. He aims to turn his estates into the City of the Sun where, before the year is out, happiness, love, and virtue will reign. Nasty [the leader of the poor] warns Goetz that the German soil will bleed if he gives all his property away. His misguided magnanimity will merely lead to slaughter. This is incomprehensible to Goetz; good cannot beget evil. But it does. What the rich young man was exhorted to do by Jesus, but which he left undone, Goetz would appear to do, and the result is disaster upon disaster. Everywhere, and without any preparation, the peasants rise up tumultuously against the barons and are crushed. The barons invade what were formerly Goetz's estates and murder the peasants.

A year and a day from Goetz's decision to forsake criminality and give saintliness a try, Heinrich appears, attended by an invisible devil, to execute a reckoning. But it is too easy an undertaking since, before they have even begun, Goetz is already halfway towards siding with Heinrich. This disconcerts Heinrich, who had envisaged it otherwise: Goetz hung with roses that he would have torn off him, and Goetz with a glint of triumph in his eyes that he, Heinrich, would have extinguished. He was to have brought Goetz to his knees—it was for that he had prepared himself. But the pride and audacity are gone—Goetz is half dead, and the pleasure of seeing him exposed and destroyed is limited. Goetz is only too aware that his good deeds were translated into corpses the moment the peasants came into contact with them. In a single day his virtue brought twenty-five thousand casualties on his head, more than in all his thirty-five years of evildoing. His attitude of mind, his intentions—not even they are things he is prepared to defend. He gives up. When he was evil, the good seemed close at hand, but when he reached out after it, it evaporated. The good is a mirage; the good is impossible.

The warped nature of Goetz's mode of proceeding does not lie in the fact that a deed envisaged as good should produce adverse consequences, for that is simply the risk one takes and it cannot be eliminated. The warpedness lies, rather, in the fact that Goetz refuses to take those conditions into account, to factor them into his calculations so as to be able to identify the acts that carry the least risk of adverse consequences, even though risk cannot be eliminated. To achieve that, he would have to make the peasants' lot a starting premise. But he does not—out of sheer religiosity. He does not relinquish his possessions for the sake of the peasants but because he wants to do, not just good, but absolute good. It is not the poverty and oppressed condition of the peasants that moves him and leads to his resigning his estates. It is not the peasants' lot and his desire to improve it that prompt his action; nor are his donations the means at his disposal by which he might change their conditions. It is the other way round. Having opted for absolute good, he asks himself, as it were, what an act in which absolute good is manifest would look like. He is not led by the needs of the people to whom he is already bound; he gives no thought to their situation even though they are those towards whom his action is directed. Unconstrained by other people, he allows a religious consideration alone—not policy—to determine the form his act shall take. Goetz's choice both of the good and of the act through which its realization is sought is a choice that floats free of situation and world. The question is solely: what action would bear the hallmark of absolute good? Answer: that action through which a person divests himself of all that he owns. Ergo, he performs it, and through the power of the good the peasants must willy-nilly be its recipients. It is not for the peasants' sake that Goetz gives away his estates but because doing so constitutes an action the goodness of which is absolute. Goetz's action is a matter concerning himself and the absolute, not himself and the peasants. When, at the end, the reckoning is made, there is mutual exasperation on the parts of both Goetz and Heinrich;

mutual accusations follow thick and fast, the one self-reproach outbidding the other. Goetz reproaches himself for being munificent simply in order to raise his inheritance and smash it to the ground, reducing it to shards. The poor were the victims, since he made it look as though he was bestowing his possessions upon them, while in fact he despised them. He used their gratitude to subjugate them. Earlier, he had ravished souls through torture, now he was doing so by means of the good. This is exaggeration, and yet is not exaggeration. Goetz has in fact pressed his good deeds upon the poor—deeds that sprang not from a feeling for their adversity but from his obsession with absolute good, with the fate of those who suffer as a result of his benefaction set at naught. In the same conversation he also admits to simply mimicking virtue. And there is something in that. When an agent chooses to perform an action not because he is driven by a strong sense of the other's need, but because the action bears the hallmark of absoluteness, as was the case with Goetz's renunciation of his estates, the act is simply a mimicry of the good.

Of the sacrifice to which he is converted in the latter half of the play, Goetz could say what he had previously said of his wickedness: There is only God and himself; everything else and everyone else are phantoms. To perpetrate an enormity he has no need of others, except for the sole purpose of being his victims. Nor, to perpetrate a monstrous good, to sacrifice himself, does he need others—at least not for any purpose beyond offering him resistance and tempting him.

Goetz is unaware that the performance of a good deed is reserved to those whose attitude of mind lies hidden beneath policy deliberations about what is best for a fellow human being—the term "policy" being used in the broadest sense. The agent's attitude of mind is a matter for the individual and God, hidden from others, something that Kierkegaard knew and yet was able to forget. If the individual is set upon accomplishing the absolute and manifest good, the good becomes the mirror image of evil. This is what Sartre seeks to convey through the narrative of his play. As far as that goes, he is right. Just as the madness in Goetz's wickedness lay in the fact that, because of it, God was supposed to fear for himself, the madness in Goetz's goodness is that God has to be immediately present to it.

It comes so easily to the theologian to speak of the infiniteness, unconditionality, and radicalness of the [ethical] demand and of the good. But it is not as simple as that. There is an absolute goodness not vouchsafed human beings—should they seek to attain it, its consequences will be indistinguishable from those of wickedness. Goetz takes his wickedness to extremes, making it monstrous so that it can draw infinity from God's infinity. Infinity is what Goetz has to have in his life if he is to have any sense of being alive; without it he is nothing. But it is the same with goodness. That too exists solely to save him from being reduced to nothing. Lacking everything, he needs infinity to fill out existence, nothing less will do; and it can only be attained through a feat, an achievement which bears the hallmark of infinity, and sacrifice alone does that. If a person is to have the imprint of eternity stamped upon his life, because without eternity his life is a desolation, he must devise an action that he feels in himself represents eternity.

It is not only through Goetz but also through Hilda, Goetz's sweetheart in the second half of the play, that Sartre wants to say that Christianity makes the good absolute and that the absolute turns the good into a corruptive power both for the agent who practices it and for those who suffer as a result of the good actions. Such actions confer benefits and happiness upon our neighbor only if they proceed on terms that are a-religious, purely human. Hilda, who has abandoned faith in God, is capable of doing good. With bitterness, Goetz says to himself that no matter whether he does good or evil, he makes himself hated. But Hilda is loved. Why? She does not act differently from Goetz, she reserves nothing for herself, she gives everything away, she helps everyone. Goetz thinks there must be more to this than meets the eye, but fails to comprehend that the crucial difference resides in the fact that Hilda acts for the sake of the poor, while he acts for the sake of an idea.

Today we often hear the theological claim, for which Kierkegaard can take the credit, to the effect that the radical ethical demand is without content. To invest it with content to the effect that we must have a care about the life of the neighbor is to humanize the demand. To this it must be replied that when devoid of content, the demand is obeyed for its own sake and the resultant action is cold, religious self-affirmation, even if obedience to it consists in renunciation and sacrifice.

The idea of absolute good can take one of two forms: it can either be realized in sociopolitical institutions or it involves setting at naught life as lived in human society. If Goetz's fanaticism, his vision of institutionalizing the Kingdom of God in what he refers to as the City of the Sun, fails to connect with any present-day theological thinking, the idea of doing absolute good through setting at naught what belongs to this world is, by contrast, in the ascendancy. On Kierkegaard's view, eternity must descend and infinity be captured in one single determinate act, namely, by helping the neighbor to love God. All other deeds bear no relation to the ethico-religious sphere. Never has the ethical so closed in on itself and closed itself off from the world as in Kierkegaard. What Hermann Broch calls the ethical qua closed system finds its extreme religious expression in Kierkegaard.

VI. Conformity and the collision between faith in God and the neighbor

The individual wants to be himself without God and the neighbor. He makes the fulfillment of his own desires and aspirations his idol, with others, time after time, suffering the consequences of it. His own godlessness brings him into conflict with his neighbor.

Kierkegaard gives due consideration to idolatry in relation to the temporal, which he refers to as relating in absolute terms to the relative. But that so doing is often to the detriment of the neighbor is not something about which he spares much thought. He is more concerned with the fact that, in their idolatrous relation to the temporal, people reach agreement on terms dictated by conformity. People relate in absolute terms to the relative in the same ways, they are of like mind regarding them, and each lets his life be determined by the other. In a word, being lost in wickedness towards the neighbor hardly figures at all for Kierkegaard as compared to losing oneself in conformity.

Kierkegaard has, therefore, no sense of faith in God being able to restore a person's life in such a way that his expressions of life gladden and benefit the other. For Kierkegaard, faith in God does not consist in the individual's realizing his life with the other in the expressions of life given him by God to that end, and which serve the good of the other.

This all springs from the fact that while he gives very little thought to the conflict with the neighbor into which the individual's godlessness plunges him, Kierkegaard gives copious thought to the conflict with the neighbor into which his faith in God plunges him. Worse than the conflict between godlessness and the neighbor is the conflict between faith in God and the neighbor. Any non-conflictual relation with the neighbor is, for Kierkegaard, conformity, and in the final analysis only one thing accomplishes a break-out from conformity, and that is the unremitting and irremediable clash with the loved one to which faith in God gives rise.

Admittedly, Kierkegaard distances himself from the idea that the work of faith should be one of loveless obedience. Without a lively love of the neighbor, the work is not one of faith. This is insisted upon again and again as early as in *Fear and Trembling,* only with the amplification that love, to be Christian, must consist in a grieving over the impossibility of realizing the fellowship with the neighbor within which it is the nature of love to reside. Christian love is a love that is out of its true element; it is sustained and vivified by the anguish associated with its inability to achieve its realization. Christian love is love bereft of fellowship.

According to Kierkegaard, God has no part in human mercy, goodness, solidarity. God does not work through what humanity has been given but only through that which, despite what they have been given, God is able to compel in humans through his demand. In the human world, God is only present to the deed which—because it runs counter to all human possibilities—bleeds from the stigmata of infinity.

VII. The sovereign expressions of life and the question of whether the will is free or constrained

Like Luther, Kierkegaard rejects the notion of a free will. But for Kierkegaard, a further issue imposes itself, namely, the battle against determinism. He has to engage in combat on two fronts, contending not only against the conception of a disengaged free will but also against determinism. And to wage war on two fronts he needs the distinction, of which Luther was innocent, between the freedom of the will and the freedom of existence. In introducing his conception of the latter, Kierkegaard sets himself in opposition both to the notion of a free will and to determinism. While Luther takes exception to the notion of a free will on the basis of his conception of the will, Kierkegaard does so on the basis of his conception of freedom. By turning inwards, *The Concept of Anxiety* tells us, the individual discovers freedom: not the abstract volitional freedom to choose this or that, but the freedom that the individual is in himself, and which he uses to render himself unfree, and to live in guilt. What Kierkegaard—in his opposition to determinism—is anxious to show is that the individual has himself to blame for his unfree life, since his existence is freedom.

If we ask wherein the freedom of existence resides for Kierkegaard, the answer is, by living as directed by eternity and the beyond. But even though, on Kierkegaard's conception of it, so living is a sheer positive, nothing positive can be said about it since the individual has severed himself from eternity and lives with that loss in unfreedom and guilt. What is of moment for human beings, which is to say of infinite moment, is the absolute alone—or the idea, as Kierkegaard also calls it—and the absolute or the idea lies beyond human existence. What has empirical existence is and remains indifferent. Is this also true of trust, mercy, and sincerity, understood in human terms? Indeed so, since, strictly speaking, the expressions of life have no claim on us, seeing that their realization redounds to our benefit.

Unlike Kierkegaard, I hold that there is much to be said, both of a positive and of an empirical nature, about the freedom of existence (to use Kierkegaard's expression)—for it consists in the sovereign expressions of life. The principal thrust behind Kierkegaard's concern with the absolute, with the idea, is that the absolute makes a claim on us that is imperative and not up for negotiation. But this is precisely the claim made by the sovereign expressions of life, in virtue of the fact that they are definitive and resist qualification. Taking up Kierkegaard's own concepts to use them against him: What he is aiming at in his talk of the absolute, the idea, is to be sought in empirical reality, in the sovereign expressions of life.

But my differences with Kierkegaard do not end there. Human life is not sheer unfreedom since the sovereign expressions of life are indeed realized, they assert themselves. Were that not so, we would not come off as well as we do in our common life. That we do so can only be because we live off something that we cannot credit to ourselves. The sovereign expressions of life are not the achievement of the will. On the contrary, when the expression of life overwhelms self-enclosedness, it is because the expression of life, and not the will, is sovereign.

Just as Kierkegaard maintained that if existence were not freedom, human beings would not be guilty, I for my part would maintain that were it not for the presence of the sovereign expressions of life, no guilt would attach to our self-enclosedness. But there my agreement with Kierkegaard ends. In contrast to him, I contend that guilt springs from the fact that wickedness feeds off goodness. If goodness did not exist for wickedness to be parasitic upon, there would be no such thing as guilt. Precisely because we have known the positive experience of the freedom of existence in the realized sovereign expressions of life, and yet flout that experience and close in on ourselves, the unfreedom of self-enclosedness is guilt and wickedness. Kierkegaard casts a blight upon human existence, rendering everything in it inconsequential, with the result that guilt becomes so comprehensive as to lack every concretion, and ends as the individual's incapacity to sustain a sense of guilt. I shall return to this.

Johannes Møllehave has leveled against me an objection to the effect that if the sovereign expressions of life do indeed exist, their realization is a matter for the individual's free will, confounding his self-enclosedness. He invokes Kierkegaard in his support, but to no avail. If I stand convicted by Møllehave's objection, so does Kierkegaard. If Møllehave says to me: If the human person is endowed with sovereign expressions of life, his will must be free—he must likewise say to Kierkegaard: If the human person's existence is freedom, his will must be free. But even without his appeal to Kierkegaard, Møllehave's objection fails. The sovereign expression of life precedes the will; its realization takes the will by surprise. It is one of those offerings in life which, to our good fortune, preempt us, and in whose absence we should be unable to carry on from one day to the next. The fact that we do so, our wickedness notwithstanding, is something Møllehave is unable to explain once he has discounted the sovereign expressions of life.

Either the will, allowing itself to be overmastered, surrenders to the expression of life, or it relies on its own efforts, and through morality's ersatz action we do what we surmise the sovereign expression of life would have done had it preempted our volition. Or else we corrupt the sovereign expression of life by, for instance, crediting ourselves with what the sovereign expression of life achieves and thus, flattering our will, we deprive the former of its sovereignty. This, then, is another way in which self-enclosedness, now in the guise of self-righteousness, is parasitic upon the sovereign expression of life.[1] The sovereign expression of life is thus not concealed by selfishness or stifled by self-enclosedness. The power so to conceal does not lie within our volition. Admittedly, I once thought that this power should be conceded to the latter when in *The Ethical Demand* (in the section "The wickedness of human beings and the goodness of life") I claimed that natural love and trust are "constructs" with which we operate "speculatively." Ole Jensen has criticized this claim, and I fully endorse his criticism, which produced clarity. For it will not do, Ole Jensen points out, simply to draw a parallel between the ethical demand and the sovereign expression of life.[2] To be sure, it is the sovereign expressions of life and their works that are demanded, but the difference between the ethical demand and the sovereign expression of life "lies precisely in the realization." The demand is unfulfillable, the sovereign expression of life is not produced by the will's exerting itself to obey the demand. The sovereign expression of life is indeed realized, but spontaneously, without being demanded. The demand makes itself felt when the sovereign expression of life fails, but without engendering the latter; the demand demands that it be itself superfluous. The demand is the correlate of sin; the sovereign expression of life is that of freedom.

There is a further point to which Ole Jensen draws attention. If we consider life to be utter equivocality, and if we regard that equivocality as the result of human iniquity, we attribute to ourselves and to our iniquity a truly stupendous power—which we do not have. To be sure, there are no limits to our iniquity, but there are limits to the devastation it can effect; which limits are evidenced by our inability to prevent the sovereign expressions of life from forcing their way through and realizing themselves. This does not mean that the grace of existence in the expressions of life renders the grace of the gospel superfluous. On the contrary, precisely because, through their realization, we are acquainted with the sovereign expressions of life and have experienced their freedom, we are without excuse when we persist in living closed in on ourselves and doing as we please in our unfreedom.

VIII. Engaging with the situation through the sovereign expressions of life

There is another peculiarity to note that attaches to the sovereign expressions of life: the claim they have on you is non-negotiable. If you are not fully at one with them, you are the reverse. If you compromise sincerity the very least, you fall into insincerity. If your fidelity is in the least qualified, you fall into infidelity. In a trice, light becomes dark. Corresponding to the radicalness of the ethical demand is the fact that the modes of existence through which alone it can be obeyed are intrinsically whole. Another thing is that what passes for sincerity, mercy, and fidelity is often only insincerity, unmercifulness, and infidelity, constrained by the pressure of external prescriptions to cloak itself in the performance of actions that are normally expressive of sincerity, mercy, and fidelity. But when what is demanded is not external, prescribed actions but—upping the ante—the whole person, it must be that the demand is obeyed with what life is in itself. Obedience can never be an integral whole unless realized through the life-possibilities already vouchsafed the individual; they are the correlates of the demand. The naked will to obedience will never render obedience an integral whole. To be obedient, the individual has to be more than obedient: he has to be sincere, merciful, faithful. The demand does not bring about the possible modes of existence through which it is to be obeyed. They are there already.

Setting aside those cases where existence presents perplexities that the individual is reluctant to recognize because of an ingrained character flaw, our task is not, as an abstract and negative self, to appropriate existence and the conditions it presents, but to engage with the interpersonal situation through the sovereign expressions of life.[3] Kierkegaard is mistaken in thinking that the escape from desire and pleasure's immediate attachment to the world calls for an effort of reflection in which the individual recalls to mind the infinite and eternal in himself, and becomes an abstract and negative self. The immediacy with which the individual is bound to the world through desire and pleasure is matched by the immediacy with which he is bound to the world through such sovereign expressions of life as trust, mercy, and the openness of speech. And since the sovereign expressions of life make claims on the individual—claims that are non-negotiable because the expressions of life are definitive and not subject to qualification—the individual is already, through his immediate embeddedness in the world, subject to a radical demand. The tussle between desire and trust, between pleasure and mercy, is played out in that immediacy. It is there that it begins.

Kierkegaard is mistaken in thinking that the infinite movement of resignation is needed for the individual to be able to apprehend himself in his eternal truth. He is mistaken in thinking that the ethical task consists in concerning oneself at every moment of one's earthly life with the winning of one's identity and becoming a self by using every instant of time to relate oneself to eternity. That concern is one of which the human person is free. Winning one's identity and becoming a self is something the individual should let happen unawares, by leaving it to the sovereign expressions of life. Eternity has incarnated the demand it imposes upon us in the interpersonal situation and in the sovereign expressions of life that correspond to it. Eternity incarnates itself not, in the first instance, in Jesus of Nazareth, but already in creation and the universality of the demand. Christianity itself contends that the idea of creation is not a peculiarly Christian notion, and it is a Christian contention that the radical demand is not a peculiarly Christian demand. Kierkegaard's thought was that eternity creates the self in the human being for eternity by situating it in the movements of infinity—through which, driven by infinite despair, the self severs itself from eternity. In this, Kierkegaard was correct, but what he ignored was the fact that eternity creates the self not only for eternity but for the neighbor too, by investing it with the sovereign expressions of life as possibilities that correspond to the claims in which eternity incarnates itself in the interpersonal situation.

If the interpersonal situation is engaged with, this engagement is mediated through the sovereign expression of life. Only when it is the conditions of existence that have to be appropriated can the subject who has to appropriate them with some justice be called an abstract and negative self, since then the individual, resisting the appropriation of his concretion, has, in thought, separated himself from it. The resisting subject is conceived as an abstract and negative self.

Does the subject engaging with the interpersonal situation never think of itself as an abstract and negative self? Yes indeed, if one shrinks from the situation and reflection sets in and one is faced with a choice. When the situation becomes a moral one, the self thinks abstractly and negatively about itself, since the situation becomes a moral one when the sovereign expressions of life fail to materialize. This is something to which I shall return.

A hypothetical objection needs to be considered. Earlier [in section V] I said that it is madness to distill eternity into a definitive act. Now I say that eternity incarnates itself in the claim that proceeds from the existence of the other and in the corresponding definitive expressions of life. Does that not amount to a flagrant contradiction? No. Generally speaking, what applies to the sovereign expression of life does not apply to the deed. In a crucial respect, the definitiveness attaching to the expression of life is the antithesis of the definitiveness attaching to the act. The expression of life does not permit deeds to be pointed out to it that it must perform whatever the circumstances. On the contrary, it sees and listens its way towards what, in the given circumstances, can be done to turn the situation round. The expression of life is what kindles the deliberations of the imagination and the intellect about what to say and do. To prescribe a particular action is to get things the wrong way round and by so doing kill off the expression of life. It is sovereign, it admits of no determination. Definitive although it may be, its realization consists least of all in some conventionally marked-out course.

Since the sovereign expression of life aims at changing the given situation and delivering the neighbor from external need or, as the case may be, the obsessive course of emotionally laden thought, eternity can incarnate itself in it. But to nail eternity to a definitive deed is, by contrast, a religious perversion of temporality: even were the deed the godliest of all, so doing would only make matters worse.

IX. The disappearance of the ethics of custom, conformism, and the relational duplication of the spirit

When the accepted morality[4] as laid down in custom and convention loses its persuasive power, reflection sets in. The moral credentials of morality are questioned, it is subjected to criticism from the perspective of a new and different understanding of what is good or bad—one at variance with that which comes to expression in time-honored morality. It may be that the old morality has become so much a matter of externals, so etiolated and fusty, that it calls out for criticism even in the absence of anything to take its place. However that may be, time was when the collective, society and religion, vouched for morality; now it is up to the individual.

But pari passu, something else happens too. There is more to the upheaval that such a fresh departure brings. When the established morality begins to crumble, the change does not merely consist in the replacement of the old duties by a new set of rules that assume their authority. The displacement goes deeper than that. The moral stance does not simply assume a new and different content but its very structure changes. When public morality loses its purchase, it results not only in the individual finding himself freely situated vis-à-vis a moral content bequeathed by tradition, but in his finding himself freely situated vis-à-vis morality as such. It is not simply a matter of weighing up the duties that had hitherto held sway, but concerns duty itself. It is the very question of moral commitment as an individual that is in the balance, and this manifests itself in the shift from talking about duties in the plural to talking about duty in the singular. In other words, just as it becomes a task for the individual to determine what moral content he will accept, so, by the same token, it becomes a task for him to decide whether or not to regard his life as something that makes claims on him. When the duties dictated by custom lose their sway, the result is not simply that the individual begins casting about for some other system of conventional duties. Rather, the question arises as to whether anything at all attaches to the idea of the individual being under moral obligation, or, if it does, why it does. The question manifests itself in a duplication: Who says we are to live under moral obligation when convention no longer does? In Hegel's formulation: Have I a duty to duty? Morality becomes spirit in a duplication. Hegel draws attention to this and Kierkegaard concurs.

The shift from *Sittlichkeit* (ethics) to *Moralität* (morality), to use Hegel's terminology, is appraised differently in empiricism and idealism, respectively. What is important for empiricism is that a deontological approach yields to, or is supplemented by, a teleological approach. Primitive ethics is deontological: there are strict duties, taboos, customs, and

demands. Behavior not conforming to the prescribed norms is condemned. There is no room for criticism of the moral code. As Stephen
Toulmin puts it, the harmonization of members' wishes and acts is ro-
bustly ordered. But, Toulmin continues, sooner or later some of the principles will be found to be in conflict with one another, or members will
become aware of the morals of other peoples, or society itself evolves. For
one reason or another the code begins to be questioned. The recognition
takes hold that members of society have a right to criticize reigning practices and to propose changes. A fresh phase in ethical development is in-
augurated. Now *motives* for action and the *outcomes* of social practices are
weighed, and people no longer simply adhere to the letter of the law. The
deontological code is supplemented by a teleological one, which provides
a measure for the criticism of the former (Stephen Toulmin, *The Place of
Reason in Ethics* [Cambridge, 1953], 137–143).

In its view of that shift, idealism, unlike empiricism, remains within a
deontological conception of ethics, indeed, it insists upon it. The duty to
duty is grounded in the claim that human persons stand in relation to the
absolute. With the collapse of morality, ideality is discovered, as Kierkegaard puts it. This is the achievement of Socrates and Plato.

In his free and admirable rendering of Kant, Hegel says that morality
transcends virtue, ethics, integrity, and so on, and does so by dint of being
distinguished by reflection. Morality is a determinate consciousness of
what duty requires and action based on that consciousness, which accordingly precedes it. Of his own volition, freely, the human person has set
duty as that which he wills. It is the duty to duty, duty for duty's sake and
its fulfillment, for which, through morality and the reflection it involves,
the individual decides. Its adoption as a rule of conduct, and compliance
with it, proceed from a freely formed conviction. For Kant, the foundation
was reason, which relates to itself in its own absoluteness, which is, as such,
freedom. Hegel expresses this by saying that Kant made self-consciousness,
which discovers itself to be infinite and knows itself as such, foundational.
This represents a turning point in modern philosophy, as Hegel recognizes. His divergence from Kant, which springs from the fact that Kant
slid back into affirming the antithesis between abstract universality and
the sensuous particular, I shall not consider here (Hegel, *Vorlesungen über
die Aesthetik,* in *Sämtliche Werke,* Bd. 12 [Stuttgart, 1953], 85–95).

As already noted, the notion of the relational duplication of the spirit emerges when the dominant ethics, qua custom and convention, begins to crumble, and subjective thought seeks morality in the idea. That, at least, was how Hegel saw it, and so did Kierkegaard in his interpretation of Platonism. But the undermining of shared codes of conduct takes place only at specific junctures in the history of the world, and once it has occurred in the history of a people and a society, a return to a primitive ethics of custom, underpinned by religion, ceases to be an option. But does this mean that all and sundry inevitably live in a relational duplication of spirit? Not at all: the life that is lived primordially and continues for the most part is that of the masses. Others determine one's life. In short, what fills the vacuum yielded by the decaying, religious, ethics of custom is conformism. Just as a life lived in the relational duplication of spirit emerged in the time of crisis following the collapse of the ethics of custom, so such a life continues to be our task, now vis-à-vis conformism. This is how Kierkegaard frames the issue.

Characteristic of the epoch in which we live is the fact that the shift from the ethics of custom to morality has become permanent. We are constantly querying and challenging the norms that we today call custom and convention, ready at every turn to put them to the test. We assume that the norms are in a constant state of flux. We live in an age of reflection, as Hegel said; the morality we know is that distinguished by reflection. The permanence of that shift means that today, too, ethical bearings are sought in one or other of two places: either, as with empiricism, in a teleological approach, or, as with existentialism, in what lies beyond this life.

In my judgement, however, ethical contexts are not well illuminated if one contents oneself with a concentration on the tension between the radical ethical demand and juridical, moral, and conventional norms: between the abstract, undetermined self and the ethics of custom. A third phenomenon has a part to play: the sovereign expressions of life.

Hegel and Kierkegaard are incorrect in thinking that once the ethics of the community has been undermined, the existence of the good or the recognition of it are conditional upon human capacities for abstraction, for thinking in generalities, for relating to the idea, with a relational duplication of the spirit being required for the attainment of the ethical. In any given situation, before duty can begin to be relevant, the spontaneous expression of life—trust, mercy, sincerity, and so on—is called forth. Not that it is a matter of engaging with the expression of life, as though it were *that* we needed to relate to. So doing would be tantamount to turning it into a duty with the duplication to which duty gives rise, as Hegel and Kierkegaard correctly observe. No, the call to us is to engage with the situation—through the corresponding sovereign expression of life. As the story comes down to us, it was not a question of the Good Samaritan engaging with his own mercifulness in his exercise of it as his duty; rather, in his mercifulness, he took charge of the man who had been set upon and lay wounded by the roadside. What occupied the Samaritan's thoughts (if we simply take the story as it stands) were the needs of the victim and how best to help him. We are told nothing of the Samaritan's relating to his own mercifulness in a recognition that it was something he was duty-bound to show.

But we can easily amplify the story and imagine that the Samaritan was tempted in the same way as were the priest and the Levite and, eschewing engagement with the situation, needed to overcome his resistance by letting the duty to duty enter as a fresh and necessary motive. In the deliberations prompted by the temptation to pass by and leave the assault victim to his fate, the Kantian Samaritan pauses to consider mercy as a duty, which may result in his conveying the assault victim to the inn and tending his wounds not from mercy but from duty. And when the agent is merciful out of duty, without being driven by mercifulness, then duty is done for duty's sake, as Hegel rightly says. But what he is certainly not right in saying is that this is morality in the best sense of the word; on the contrary, it is morality as a substitute, and there is no other morality. Granted, it is better than brutality or indifference, but it is inferior to the immediate realization of mercy's sovereign expression of life. Duty enters when I am trying to wriggle out of the situation.

The duty to duty enters, then, in two, or if you will, three, contexts: when the ethics of custom crumbles away, when we are uneasy with our own conformism, and when what is to be achieved through action proves insufficient to motivate it and an additional motive is needed. The duplication of which Hegel and Kierkegaard speak also arises when duty has to fill a motivational gap if the action is to be realized at all.

X. Morality is the delivery of substitute motives to substitute actions

The sovereign expressions of life, being spontaneous, are pre-moral. Our attitude of mind is inseparable from what we seek to bring about through our agency since the motivational state consists in purposing the result of our agency. There is no point in asking whether a merciful act is good in itself without considering its outcomes. Such separation is impossible: a term like "merciful" is at once a characterization both of the attitude of mind and of the intention informing the act. Mercifulness is elicited by the perception of another person being hampered in the realization of his life. It appeals to as elemental a hope as that of seeing every life realized. The other person's lot is at odds with that hope, and from the dissonance inherent in that circumstance is born the mercifulness that seeks, through action, to vindicate the hope and remove what stands in the way of its fulfillment—whether the obstacles be poverty, need, oppression, or exploitation.

From a philosophical point of view, the neglect of ethically descriptive phenomena gives rise to pseudo-problems, with one such being the conflict between the ethics centered on attitude of mind and that centered on goods. With a phenomenon such as mercy, that problem cannot so much as arise in that the relevant disposition is triggered by the other's misfortune and consists simply in an effort to transform his situation. Kant could only arrive at his ethics of duty by disparaging all ethically descriptive phenomena as inclinations, and Kierkegaard, for his part, only by ignoring all sovereign expressions of life.

Duty is not a phenomenon that can subsist on its own; it is merely a motive which demands to be realized in some action which the agent remains reluctant to perform until the motive is strong enough. Mercy exists only as realization, an act that is motivated by what it seeks to bring about.

Once an action is declared to be a duty, the separation of motive and effect, mental disposition and outcome, has begun. The effects and outcomes in question begin to fade into the background to be replaced by a focus on the motive and its reinforcement. The act that is turned into a

duty is the act we are tempted not to perform; we are reckoning with inclinations that are powerful and that seek to deflect us from the action. Our
interest in the consequences of the action proves insufficiently strong; it
loses momentum. It is then that duty has to leap into the breach and ensure that the act is still performed. Duty contrives this not by seeking to
reinforce our attachment to what the action is intended to achieve, but
by supplying a fresh motive. That is important. When we turn an act into
a duty we discount the motivation that consists in our being gripped by
the objective of the action. We no longer count on our caring enough to
get the thing done. The same applies to virtue, in that the motivation
for which it is the disposition, namely, the thought and the sense of the
rightness of the action, is a substitute for an engagement in what will be
achieved through one's action, which is the only natural and genuine motive. Just as duty is a substitute motive, virtue is a substitute disposition.
Morality exists to deliver substitute motives to substitute actions because
the sovereign and spontaneous expressions of life, with their attachment
to what the act is intended to achieve, either fail to materialize or are
stifled.

In duty and virtue, the individual's connection to others, to society,
and to the world is loosened: the thought of and sense of the rightness of
the act are given independent status and are interposed. Granted, the result of the action is not ignored, for, since the agent knows that achieving
the outcome is indispensable, duty and virtue come into play; but the motive is no longer drawn from the consequences that the action will have for
the lives of others and for society, but is sought in the individual himself.
When motivation is divorced from the intended outcome, the individual
is thrown back upon himself where motivation is concerned. Duty and
virtue are moral introversions.

When the intended outcome of the act constitutes its motivation, that
motivation consists in spontaneous expressions of life. That is why efforts
to evolve a disposition that will produce such motivations and secure the
performance of the relevant actions are unfeasible. The spontaneity of motivation makes it impossible. The establishing and fixing of duty and virtue is not something that can be worked at. Only reflection on motivation
is amenable to such efforts. The agent reflects on the rightness of the act
in order to do it for the sake of its rightness—and not for the sake of
its results.

But what, then, is the sentiment evoked by the thought of the rightness of the act? It is easy to imagine that it would be one of rapture at one's own righteousness. The question is whether it can be anything else. It can indeed, say Kant and Kierkegaard. Couched in Kantian terms, the relation to the noumenal world cancels out what is here referred to as moral introversion, and reverence for the law precludes self-righteousness from acting as the motivating sentiment. Couched in Kierkegaardian terms, the relation to infinity and eternity represents not introversion but interiorization, and duty and virtue are replaced by decision. To put it perspicuously, albeit crudely: once motivation has been decoupled from the intended outcomes of the action, Kant and Kierkegaard deem it susceptible of a religious determination, with the result that the will, to speak with Kant, or obedience, to speak with Kierkegaard, becomes the only thing that is good in itself.

But then Kant and Kierkegaard have forgotten that it is of the nature of morality to be a substitute. Their respective ethics amount to a religious sublimation of the thinking that cleaves to the moral substitute.

Jørgen K. Bukdahl has put the question to me, partly as an objection, whether, in some sense or other, the individual does not have to "commit himself to" the sovereign expressions of life. There is a spontaneity of decisiveness, he says, by which he means that not only is the expression of life spontaneous but so too is decision. Bound up with the sovereign expression of life must be "oneself vouching for it," "oneself being integral to it," he says.

But what is meant by a spontaneous decision? Perhaps a comparison between a decisiveness in favor of a definitive expression of life such as trust or mercifulness and decisiveness in relation to duty will shed light. In one particular respect, the relevant decisiveness is different in each case.[5]

To decide to show trust or mercifulness is to decide to surrender oneself to trust or mercy. Trust and mercifulness must be there already as life-possibilities. If they are not, no decision can elicit them. So the expression "to decide to show trust or mercifulness" is somewhat inadequate, but it is not incorrect because the decision consists in the renunciation of attitudes or movements of thought and feeling that are incompatible with trust and mercifulness—such as, for example, aloofness, guardedness, reticence, glibness, vengefulness, arrogance. The spontaneity accruing to the decision springs from the spontaneous expression of life—trust, mercifulness, sincerity, and so forth—to which the person decides to give free rein.

By contrast, no inadequacy attaches to the expression "deciding to do one's duty." Duty is self-governance and corresponds to the self-governance a decision represents. There is no such thing as surrendering to one's duty. On the contrary, in duty I make myself master of everything that allures me and tempts me to neglect my duty. Thus it is that I can enlist duty as a substitute motive and do what trust or mercy would have done had they been present. I am not in control of trust and mercy to the same extent that I am of my duty.

While duty is a substitute motive, freedom is not even that. Kierkegaard says of the freedom that constitutes the individual that it is constantly preoccupied solely with itself. Indeed, what distinguishes it from *liberum arbitrium* is determinable by reference to that feature: while *liberum arbitrium* relates to something external to the individual, the freedom that is the individual relates to itself. This makes it impossible for freedom to be a motive to action, something Kierkegaard seems not to have considered.

Let us imagine that, in a particular situation that calls for the performance of a concrete act, the individual reflects upon his freedom to act. The act enjoined by the situation is uncongenial to him; he performs it only with reluctance but concedes that he has the freedom to perform it. But even as he begins to reflect, a paralysis sets in. The individual has stepped out of the concrete situation and entered into himself, so to speak. Granted, the situation and the opportunity to act still obtain, they have not been forgotten, but now they serve merely as an occasion for self-reflection. But this means that what Kierkegaard is claiming for his determination of freedom as something that relates only to itself—in effect, that this determination describes what happens when a decision is taken and acted upon—is, properly considered, a description of its very antithesis, namely, of how we shrink from action and gravitate towards a state of paralysis. Reflection on the freedom to act is never an impetus to action. On the contrary, the impetus to action comes from a consideration of the action's purpose, content, and meaning. The realization of the freedom that I myself am, and in which my existence consists, is something I can achieve only by forgetting it. Not that this is so extraordinary: while it is one thing to act, it is quite another to reflect upon the constitution of my existence as the freedom to act. Both are indeed part of my life, but it does not do to confuse their respective realizations. That an action is free does not mean that reflection on that circumstance can serve as the mainspring of action.

Notes

1. Møllehave notes further that the sovereign expressions of life exclude offence. "There is no reason to take offence at the sovereign expressions of life; instead we should all be deeply affected by them: trust, openness, mercy." That depends on how you look at it. Would one not, I wonder, have to approach one's task somewhat superficially if it is to result in one's being utterly grabbed by the sovereign expressions of life? Returning for a moment to my earlier illustration, let us imagine that Goetz von Berlichingen, offence welling up within him, asks how long he is to go on showing the traitor Weislingen trust, how many more times he is to give him a chance: he has now done so seven times and that must be enough. If Goetz von Berlichingen gets the answer that nothing less than seventy times seven will do, I wonder whether he would not take offence. No one can do other than take offence at one's task if he takes it seriously. In order to hear a demand and take offence at it, it must be unintelligible, observes Møllehave in the same context. Yes, if the offence in question were of an intellectual nature, but not if it is ethical. What is as intelligible as can be may perfectly well offend ethically. As intelligible as it is to Goetz von Berlichingen that he should give Weislingen a chance seventy times seven times, he would be equally offended if he were to take in what it meant.

2. As I did in my original reply to Møllehave in *Information* [July 30–31, 1966], which could only have been misleading.

3. Translators' note: In the Danish original, in order to stress the contrast to Kierkegaard's concept of "self-appropriation," Løgstrup, using the same verb—*at overtage*—lets it do double duty, rendered here as "appropriating" and "engaging with."

4. Translators' note: In this section Løgstrup uses the Danish terms *moral* and *moralsk* to refer indiscriminately to both traditional and reflective morality. We have translated these terms as "morality" and "moral," respectively. Establishing a link with Hegel's distinction between (traditional) *Sittlichkeit* and (reflective) *Moral*, Løgstrup also uses the Danish term *sædelighed* to designate traditional

morality. We have rendered this term as "ethics." Finally Løgstrup uses the Danish terms *etik* and *etisk* when he refers to ethical theory, which are translated as "ethics" and "ethical," respectively.

5. I am assuming that it is not an explanation of freedom that Bukdahl is after, inasmuch as I take it that he agrees with Kierkegaard that any attempt to explain freedom implies that it is an illusion, since what explanations elucidate are determining factors.

THREE

Sovereign Expressions of Life, the Golden Rule, Character Traits, and Norms

The sovereign expressions of life

At four o'clock in the morning there is an insistent ring at the door. When the woman descends the secret police are outside, demanding that she open up. Once inside, they ask for her husband. They are informed that, as it happens, he is not at home but away on business. One of the two men, the subordinate, heavily armed, ugly as sin, and looking capable of every kind of brutality, starts searching the house. The other, possessed of an engaging manner, all amiability and courtesy, is talking to the woman meanwhile and assuring her that the visit is of no consequence, merely a routine procedure. The woman acts obligingly, appearing surprised—a composed and polished performance. She is perfectly aware that his charming insistence on the insignificance of their visit is aimed solely at getting her to talk, and is not taken in by anything that he says. She knows that from the least unconsidered remark ammunition will be forged for use against her husband and herself. In spite of that—and this is probably the oddest part of the whole business—she needs constantly to rein in an inclination to talk to the man as to another human being, as though he might be drawn from his destructive enterprise to properly human perceptions and good sense. Unremittingly, she must keep a cool head. Why? What manifests itself in that inclination? Nothing other than the elemental and definitive peculiarity attaching to all speech qua spontaneous expression of life: its openness. To speak is to speak openly. This is not something the individual does with speech; it is there beforehand, as it were, qua anonymous expression of life. We yield to its sovereignty at the very moment in which we begin to speak. Even in a situation where hoodwinking the other is a matter of life or death, where the other's destructive intent is patently obvious and his strategy wholly transparent—even there, it makes itself felt, so that not speaking openly is palpably felt to be contrary to nature. The sovereign expression of life preempts us; we are seized by it. Therein lies its spontaneity. That too is illustrated by the above episode. The man from the secret police seeks to exploit the fact that openness of speech and trust preempt the woman's recognition of the intentions behind his questions and her astute calculation of the consequences her answers will have. In all their elementalness and definitiveness, the expressions of life are what normally sustain all human interaction. Indeed, this is evidenced by the fact that however interested we may be in attaining knowledge and a just estimation of whatever it is we might be talking about, we do not seek to scrutinize each other's characters and size each other up in face-to-face situations. That is something we reserve for our musings, when the others are absent and when, in calling to mind all the negative experiences we have had with them, we get vexed with them. In our musings, we are brimming over with thoughts about the people we are at odds with and the standards against which we judge their characters. Their presence, by contrast, expunges all our notions and standards, unless we seize the opportunity to have it out with them and passions run high. But otherwise there has to be an ingrained animosity or a deep-seated sense of grievance if those thoughts and standards are to persist in the presence of the other. If you are averse to losing your animosity, there is nothing for it but to stay away and nurse your musings. All this comes of the fact that the immediacy of human interaction is sustained by the immediate expressions of life, whose sovereignty is such that they defeat our past experiences and private musings.

The sovereign expressions of life and the Golden Rule

Attitude of mind and outcome of agency are inextricably intertwined in the sovereign expression of life. In that feature, too, consists its spontaneity. This is manifest in an expression of life such as mercy, which consists in removing the hindrances that hamper the flourishing of the individual in disadvantaged circumstances.[1]

Admittedly, "spontaneous" is not the most felicitous term, especially if it is associated with a bubbling, welling gush of life. Etymologically, however, the word is appropriate because it means that what persons do, they do in accordance with the nature of things and of their own accord. In other words, what persons do spontaneously they do unconstrainedly and without ulterior motives. Which is to say that by calling mercy spontaneous, we mean that acts of mercy are elicited solely by the condition or situation in which the other finds himself, without the merciful agent deriving any benefit from his deeds, not for himself nor for any third party or institution. Mercy is spontaneous because the least interruption, the least calculation, the least dilution of it in the service of something else destroys it entirely, indeed turns it into the opposite of what it is—namely, mercilessness. Spontaneity is not something of which there can be more or less; it must be all in all if the sovereign expression of life is to prevail at all. Its radicalness consists not in any masterly feat but simply in the fact that the least ulterior motive is excluded.

If the sovereign expression of life is wanting, it does not mean that we must abandon the outcome of agency to which it was directed. That can still be aimed at, except that, with the attitude of mind falling short, it is now aimed at as an outcome demanded.

As the sovereign expression of life is radical, so too will the demand be that, as it were, steps into the breach for it; so much is obvious. The demand comes to expression in, for instance, the Golden Rule: Do unto others as you would have them do unto you. This is anything but a tepid rule of reciprocity, even if, taken literally, it might seem to be such. On the contrary, it is a rule governing the use of the imagination. It requires of us that we seek to imagine how we would wish to be treated were we in the other's stead—and then that we actually go on to act towards the other in that way. Clearly, it is as radical as anything could be.

But as soon as the radicalness is transposed from the sovereign expression of life to the demand, it inescapably becomes distorted. The radicalness comes to denote the unmanageable, or what is as good as unmanageable.[2] In other words we smuggle the heroic into the radical.

Strangely enough, when the worst comes to the worst, we prefer to do the heroically unmanageable thing rather than the radically manageable. We prefer the former even when it means risking our lives in attempting it, whereas the performance of the radically manageable poses no threat to life at all.

The fear of other people is greater than the fear of death. The same individual who during an uprising or war does not shrink from taking part in actions where he puts his life at risk, shrinks from giving another person his mind if the other will take exception to it. And here I am thinking not of the mercenary nor of the war into which the conscript is forced whether he will or no, but of the respectable citizen who loves a quiet life and could well do without the war and yet, of his own volition, becomes a partisan. Albeit filled with horror at the thought of losing his life, he signs up voluntarily and defies his fear of death. The curious thing is that, afterwards, he is unable to defy his fear of other people. And I do not have in mind the exceptional case where the person to whom he submits has weighty authority and considerable power, so that one cannot, with impunity, give him a piece of one's mind. No, even when he does not harbor the least liking for the other person, perhaps considering him a fool, and even when he can say what he likes without paying for it—there, again, he shrinks from doing so. There, too, his fear of other people outstrips his fear of death.[3]

In extraordinary situations, for example during wars, many people are prepared for the extraordinary. At a point in *Der Arbeiter: Herrschaft und Gestalt* (The Worker: Mastery and Form), Ernst Jünger, the foremost advocate for the cool, impersonal heroism that is the counterpart of today's advanced technology, writes: "Here images of the highest discipline of the heart and nerves have become history—in the swirling flames of aircraft that have been shot down, in the pockets of air in sunken submarines on the floor of the sea—tests of the extreme, cool-headed, metallic aplomb that allows the heroic mind to use the body as a mere instrument, and to extract from it an array of complex services beyond the bounds of self-preservation."

There is a capacity for heroism latent in more people than we might think. But the exceptional situation is needed to call it forth. However, once that situation obtains, presenting its formidable challenge, the individual summons up all his or her physical and mental powers to square up to it. Even when the exceptional situation requires that he put his life on the line, having from the outset no chance of saving it, with death a certainty, the individual rises to the challenge.

While stressing that the radical is not the heroic, it should not be denied that there are situations in which the act that is required bears the mark of sacrifice and possibly of the ultimate sacrifice. This occurs during persecutions, for example, whether politically or religiously motivated.

But how can it be that the radical is now a sacrifice, now such a manageable affair that not the smallest sacrifice attaches to it? The answer is simple: it all depends on the event, the condition or situation, in which the other finds himself and to which one's action must conform. The radicalness does not consist in unmanageability but in spontaneity, construed as the absence of ulterior motives both immoral and moral. This has two consequences.

Since the demand inevitably generates moral ulterior motives, its radicalness, paradoxically enough, consists in demanding its own superfluity.

When the radical is not the heroic but equally often the manageable, it becomes impossible to see whether the act is performed from mercy or for the sake of the moral ulterior motive or for the sake of some other gain. To relinquish one's own interest, bending for the sake of the other, is something an individual can do from weakness or strength, from a fear of human beings or from mercy, naturally or unnaturally.

In the name of the radical demand and the Golden Rule, judgement can indeed be passed on deeds that harm others. To refrain from such actions and show proper consideration for others is as manageable as anything. Luther makes a judgement to that effect in his work on business acumen and usury, a topic to which I shall return in a later chapter on politics and economics.[4]

The sovereign expressions of life and traits of character

The presence of another individual elicits trust and sincerity from the first; the distress of the other elicits the mercy of the first. In the immediate interaction between one person and another, the sovereign expressions of life are realized. But however immediate the relationship between two parties may be, it is almost invariably also mediated by some matter. The stricken individual cannot be helped without a piece of direct work being done. Unless that work is done and done properly, mercy becomes sentimentality and rhetoric.

In the case of character traits, the order of ranking or of grounding is the reverse. In the main, the character trait comes to expression in the person's relation to some work that has to be done or a task that has to be accomplished; and only as a consequence of that does the relationship to the other person—who has an interest in the work's being done and the task's being accomplished—succeed or fail. If a dependable person is assigned a task, one can be sure that he will stick to it, will not shirk it, will apply his best efforts, will not be negligent. Whatever he commits himself to doing is in good hands since it is in his. In consequence, his relations with his fellow workers are good; they do not need to keep an eye on him.

In short, mercy is realized primarily in relation to the other person— by engaging in the work through whose execution alone the other is helped. Dependability manifests itself primarily in relation to work—and is accordingly also to the benefit of the individual's fellow workers. That is one difference. But there is another.

Since the sovereign expression of life attaches to the immediate relationship between one person and another, that is where it ends, ethically speaking, by which is meant that it cannot be subordinated to goals more remote than the intended outcome of agency that meets the other's need.

By contrast, an appraisal of the end served by the work or the task does not enter into the character trait. Ethically speaking, it does not end there, and it may very well prove to serve the purposes of destruction. There is nothing to prevent a gangster's being dependable. He will not rest until the blackmail that was his assigned task has been consummately executed, so the task is in good hands when assigned to him.

Kant would not allow that anything in the whole world is good except a good will. Neither traits of character nor what are here called the sovereign expressions of life found favor in his eyes. His argumentation for none of them counting as moral is various.

Traits of character—Kant cites courage, moderation, self-control—cannot be accounted good in the moral sense since they are only means, and so it remains uncertain whether the end to which they are means is good or evil. He is right in saying that traits of character that we consider good can be used to evil ends, but whether we should refuse them moral status on that account is another matter. Doing so has the disadvantage of being at odds with common usage, narrowing the sphere of morality, and in Kant's own work it contributed to the formalization of his ethics, investing it with an architectonic that does not withstand scrutiny.

But take instead mercy, forgiveness, sincerity, and trust, which do not permit themselves to become means to other objectives irrelevant to their own realization. They would seem to be expressions that are ethical in themselves. But Kant would not have that, either. They are rejected for another reason. They are inclinations, and inclinations are that for which gratification is sought, and the person thereby gratified is oneself. Properly considered, then, the expressions of life referred to here are egoistic. Kant's argumentation is untenable. To begin with, the concept of need, whose correlate is gratification, is going to have to be stretched considerably if the sovereign expressions of life are to be called needs. Second, the intended result is the transformation of a situation and not the pleasure—selfish pleasure, it is implied—which is produced when that transformation has been accomplished. Kant is guilty of what is known as the hedonistic fallacy.

Character traits and sovereign expressions of life can work in tandem, and they can collide. In the following sections we shall be examining their positive interaction and its relation to norms. Later on, in the section on politics and economics, we shall see how traits of character and the sovereign expressions of life can come into conflict with each other.

The positive interaction between character traits and sovereign expressions of life and the relation to norms

Moral norms, rules, precepts, principles, laws, or whatever we wish to call them, arise in and through the fact that a task needs to be performed, work needs to be carried out, the life of the community needs to be managed—because all these things certainly present difficulties to be overcome and make claims on the parties involved. Some of the exigencies draw on our physical and intellectual resources as well as our technical skill, whereas others of them are moral. Around every activity and every form of common life a set of moral rules crystallizes.

For instance, it is human nature not to be held back by the sea but to brave the element and sail it. The sea and the ship create their own morality, and it is a simple one. We are familiar with it from the tales of the Polish-born British writer Joseph Conrad; a seaman himself, he knew what he was talking about. A single line is drawn—the supreme commandment runs, Never abandon anyone or anything to save your own skin. This is a morality for *in extremis* situations. When the hurricane breaks, so that only by risking your life can you do your duty, the line is drawn. Captain MacWhirr in the story "Typhoon" is as stupid as a man can be when he knows his stuff but is completely without imagination. From sheer stubbornness, which derives from nothing other than an extraordinary lack of imagination, he steers his ship into a typhoon, and only very narrowly do the crew secure their escape with the vessel intact. But despite his positively dangerous stupidity, he is a decent enough fellow, for he is innocent of the temptation to abandon anything or anyone. Such is the morality of the sea, and he obeys it.

But even though our enterprises and our common life cannot succeed without rules (including moral rules) being complied with, this does not mean that we need to know them and have them present to our minds, despite that being the impression one might get if one reads, not novels, but accounts of ethics. Moral philosophers, no matter what their orientation, almost always entertain exaggerated conceptions of the role played by reflection on moral rules in our everyday actions and decisions. This is presumably because they simply read across from their own philosophical preoccupation with moral rules to ordinary life. This is arguably what is exemplified when one of their number, P. Nowell-Smith, whose examination of the language of morals is far from undiscerning, claims outright that the moral attitude is at its strongest in calm and reflective moments (*Ethics* [London, 1954], 230–231). One would be equally justified in asserting the contrary: that the moral attitude is never so strong as when the challenge is generated by a tense situation where things are so hectic that there is no time to reflect on the moral rules which the concrete requirements exemplify—as the philosopher claims they do. So much is certain at any rate: that reflection on the relevant moral rules is anything but a feature of every ethical situation. And this should not be taken simply to mean that the reason for our not pondering moral rules is that some particular form of moral conduct is so ingrained in us that we do what we ought out of habit. For not even when called upon to make the ultimate sacrifice does the individual need to give the moral rule a thought. It is unlikely that anyone has given his life in order to comply with a moral rule. If the task engrosses the agent, if he is drawn in by the work and caught up in the embrace of fellowship, there will be no thoughts to spare morality. A consciousness, disengaged from the concrete situation, of having to obey the one or the other moral rule does not exist. The requirements to which one conforms are fully incorporated in the actual situation and are not segregated from it to be obeyed through reflection on them qua moral items. It is with ethics as it is with logic. If we are grappling with theoretical problems and are engrossed by them, we give no thought to the rules of inference we follow.

And there is a further thing. To the execution of a task, the completion of a piece of work, and the management of life in the community, there correspond in part the sovereign expressions of life and in part such character traits as perseverance, trustworthiness, reliability, loyalty, self-criticism, fortitude, and so on. But there is a difference. The sovereign expressions of life cannot be generated through practice as character traits can. In the old days, traits of character acquired through practice were called virtues. That concept has disappeared from ethics for several reasons. Over time it became negatively laden, through virtue being pursued for its own sake. The fact was overlooked that, actually, it is the task, the work, the life of the community that create both morality and the character that respects it. The individual's character does indeed correspond to the morality he professes, although not, however, from love of morality or reflection on its dictates, but rather through involvement in the enterprises and the life of the community out of which both morality and character are born. Morality does not spring up of itself but arises out of something. And it is from the involvement in, and attachment to, that out of which morality springs that the character traits that correspond to morality are formed—and not from an interest in freestanding or free-floating moral dictates and precepts. So the words denoting the particular traits of character tell us less about what expectations we may entertain about the individual's compliance with the moral rule than they tell us how we may expect to find the individual playing his or her role in community life, performing the task, and engaging in the work for whose sake morality exists.

As mentioned above, it is of the nature of the sovereign expression of life to be motivated by the outcome at which action is aimed. Attitude of mind and intention are inseparable. This is tantamount to saying that character traits emerge through involvement in the tasks set by the living together and enterprise of humans—prior to the traits being morally sequestered from those tasks in order to be cultivated as virtues. Sovereign expressions of life and character traits may thus converge in the concrete case without its being possible to say, and without there being a need to consider, which is which.

Let me offer an illustration taken from Joseph Conrad's story *The Nigger of the Narcissus*. The Negro Jimmy Wait has been moved from the forecastle to a cabin on the deck because he is ill, and when the hurricane strikes he is forgotten. With the ship listing beyond recovery, it suddenly dawns on the crew that if Jimmy has not already drowned he must be trapped inside, since the cabin is on the side towards which the ship is listing. The boatswain and three others immediately go to get him out, and there is no slippage between their thought and action even though they are risking their lives in so doing. Having once reached the cabin from the opposite side and smashed in the wall, they drag him aft with great difficulty, because he is so unwieldy. Now and again he comes to and mutters a few words, but only to express his resentment that they had not fetched him earlier, and they are unable to rid themselves of the shocking sus-

picion that in the face of all their toil and perseverance he is just pretend-
ing to be ill. They are furious with him. Their hearts' secret and burning
desire is to rain slaps and punches down on him, and yet they treat him
tenderly all the while, as if were he made of glass. Not for any price would
they lose him.

Joseph Conrad recounts an action in which four seamen obey the
dictate of the morality of the sea without giving it the least thought: they
are too absorbed in the matter at hand for that. They have probably never,
while at sea, given the morality of the sea a thought, no more than people
ever give logic a thought when reasoning, and reasoning correctly. The
episode is illustrative because it is so grotesque. When the work allows
them the breathing space for a moral reflection, it is one of hatred towards the miserable, self-pitying malingerer with whom they are grappling. While detesting Jimmy Wait, they display all the character traits and
realize the sovereign expressions of life that correspond to the morality to
which they are committed: daring, solidarity, self-forgetfulness, but, note,
not for the sake of morality but on account of their absorption in one of
the tasks for which morality is needed and from which it springs. As Conrad's account has it, in the words of one of the crew: "[I]t had become a
personal matter between us and the sea."

A diametrically opposite attitude to one's own character traits or qualities
from that which we encounter in Joseph Conrad's seamen is portrayed in
Robert Musil's novel *The Man Without Qualities (Der Mann ohne Eigen-
schaften)*. Of the protagonist, Ulrich, his friend Walter says to his wife:

> He always knows what to do. He can gaze into a woman's eyes. He can
> exercise his intelligence efficiently on any given problem at any given
> moment. He can box. He is talented, strong-willed, unprejudiced, he
> has courage and he has endurance, he can go at things with a dash and
> he can be cool and cautious—I have no intention of examining all of
> this in detail, let him have all these qualities! For in the end he hasn't
> got them at all! They have made him what he is, they have set his
> course for him, and yet they don't belong to him. When he is angry,
> something in him laughs. When he is sad, he is up to something.
> When he is moved by something, he will reject it. Every bad action

will seem good to him in some connection or other. And it will always be only a possible context that will decide what he thinks of a thing. Nothing is stable for him . . . [E]very one of his feelings is only a point of view, and whatever a thing is, it does not matter to him what it is, it's only some accompanying 'way in which it is'.[5]

Had Ulrich been acquainted with Walter's characterization of him, he would have wholly endorsed it. He is fully aware that when he is animated and acts animatedly he is, at once, both impassioned and indifferent. Ulrich has had a go at everything and is at any moment prepared to throw himself into something new, which need not mean anything at all to him, just so long as it arouses his impulses to action. Without significant exaggeration, he can say of his life that everything that has happened in it and the personal qualities he has acquired in the course of it belong in a sense more to each other than to him.

In other words, there is in Ulrich an inner disengagement from his thoughts, feelings, and actions. He is able to use them as instruments. If I might apply a metaphor: he is the director of his own life, directing his own qualities, feelings, reactions.

Not in the sense that Ulrich is prey to the illusion that he is himself able to decide whom he will be. He does not for a moment imagine that he can construct his qualities or his fate. He accepts himself as the person he is. There is no lack of realism in his sense of himself, and he is indeed satisfied with himself the way he is. The problem is not the Kierkegaardian one of embracing the existence that is one's own without, fantastically, wanting to determine what it must be like in order that one may be willing to embrace it. On the contrary, as the most natural thing in the world, Ulrich has accepted his make-up and his life. As Walter puts it, his qualities have made him the person he is and have set his course.

But if a person makes himself the director of his qualities, his feelings and his actions, the question arises as to the identity of the author of the play in which the person directs himself. The answer is simple: the author can be none other than the existence in which the person happens to be placed. By virtue of its historical character, existence composes those experiences and situations in which the superior individual is his own director. It is indeed so, but is not the fact that the narrative of history no longer has any meaning one of the things that Robert Musil is telling us? Indeed, that it only becomes possible to be the director of one's own life when history no longer functions as the author of our lives? But then we find ourselves in a hopeless and strangely paradoxical situation, and I wonder whether it is not this that Robert Musil wants to expose. Never before have human beings so needed history as the author of their lives as at the present time, which finds them as the directors of their own existence. But that is precisely, right now, what history is not. Indeed, so pernicious is the situation that history, by failing to be the author of our lives, affords us the possibility of being the directors of our own lives while creating a need in us, greater than at any earlier time, to have it as the author of our lives.

Admittedly, it might well be said—and with justice—that both in Ulrich's life in Robert Musil's novel and in the lives of the seamen in Joseph Conrad's story, it is the task facing them that challenges their powers and it is through that task that they are tested. Nonetheless, the difference stands out. Ulrich tests himself, his character, and his powers against the task challenging him in a sporting fashion, an attitude that results in the strange dividedness in his relation to the task, which, as noted, is at once impassioned and indifferent. There is and remains, as it were, a kind of sporting detachment from the task, which in a sense mocks it. Although serving to arouse impulses to action in him, it fails to dispel his indifference, to send the director packing, and to make his engagement with the task personal. For that to happen, the task would need to have sufficient substance and import to be addressed in its historical singularity and irrevocability. But that is precisely what it does not have.

In the case of the seamen aboard *The Narcissus,* the opposite is true. There is nothing divided, sporting, or detached in their approach to the task, but it is as personal as the task is singular and their efforts or dereliction irrevocable, in that, when it comes down to it, they accept the sea and the ship which, qua author of their existence, sets them their task.

Ulrich, by contrast, assumes that we are a species of worldless individuals, ourselves the authors of our goals—as though there were not a challenge that proceeds to us from the world and its order. The ethical point of view is not a product of our aspirations but a backlighting effect that illuminates them, engendered by the basic givens of our condition which are not within our power to change.

Four stages in the development of British moral philosophy in the twentieth century

But in ethical reasoning, too, principles play a far lesser role than is often assumed. Before attempting to show this I need to give an account—in broad outline—of the development of British moral philosophy, for it is chiefly there that analyses of ethical argumentation have been conducted.

Mogens Blegvad, who traces these developments in his book *Den naturalistiske fejlslutning* (The Naturalistic Fallacy [Copenhagen, 1957]), begins with some remarks on their background in the naturalism of the nineteenth century.

Naturalism is the idea that since human beings are embedded in the universe their nature is part of the nature of the universe. Human life and consciousness are part of the natural order and are explainable by reference to the laws by which nature is governed. Naturalism recognizes no distinction between the human and the natural world. Everything is nature, and the human subject is no more dependent on anything beyond, anything transcendent, than the natural order of which it is part. That ethics belongs to human existence is explained, not through humanity's being subject to a divine or ideal demand, but by reference to the circumstance that ethics springs from human nature. Indeed, a number of naturalistic theories have been in circulation, but one of them, and by far the most dominant, was based on the assumption that human nature consists primarily in needs, so that the good is the satisfaction of need, or, as it was put, the good is the same thing as pleasure. From this it follows that only those actions are good which give rise to the greatest and most enduring pleasure—or, if the material conditions are sufficiently adverse, the least pain. The ethical quality 'good' is accordingly defined by reference to a natural phenomenon such as, for example, 'pleasure'.

Now we become acquainted with natural phenomena through sense-experience and gain insight into them by drawing on the methods of empirical science. This is also true with regard to a natural phenomenon such as pleasure. Psychology instructs us as to how it arises and is sustained. But since the quality 'good', which is the burden of ethics, is nothing but 'pleasure', investigable by an empirical science such as psychology, ethics proves to be reducible to an empirical science. From the standpoint of moral philosophy, naturalism may be defined as the conviction that the problems of ethics can be solved by means of scientific methods.

It was this naturalistic moral philosophy G. E. Moore found himself faced with and which he attacked. One of the features to which he took strong exception was the fact that the champions of the naturalistic theory did not content themselves with asserting a necessary connection between 'good' on one hand and 'maximal pleasure' on the other, so that 'good', distinct in itself, and 'maximal pleasure', distinct in itself, remained what they were, but asserted that they were identical, with 'good' not being allowed to be anything other than a synonym for 'maximal pleasure'.

Indeed, Moore's central argument against naturalism is precisely to the effect that if 'good' means nothing other than 'maximal pleasure', it becomes meaningless to ask whether one can call the action that produces maximal pleasure good. It would be the same as asking whether an action that produces maximal pleasure may be called an action that produces maximal pleasure. But since it manifestly is meaningful to ask whether maximal pleasure is what makes an action good, goodness and maximal pleasure must be two different things, and the core moral concept 'good' is not definable in terms of a nonmoral expression such as 'maximal pleasure'.

Moore goes on to assert that the error of the naturalists was to seek to define 'good' at all. For it cannot be done. 'Good', as Moore sees it, designates a property that is simple and unanalyzable. And this is not unique to 'good' but applies to many other properties—the property 'yellow' is another such. Only compound objects are definable—by reference to the properties of which they are compounded. Sooner or later in our analysis, we arrive at simple properties not susceptible of further analysis, nor, consequently, of definition. Only immediately and directly, intuitively, do we become acquainted with them and familiar with them. This applies, for instance, to a property such as 'yellow' and it applies to a property such as 'good'. Thus Moore emerges as an exponent of a version of what has been termed ethical intuitionism—the first stage in the development of moral philosophy in the twentieth century.

Moore's view did not go unchallenged, however. The moral philosophers who came after him did not, as he had done, confine themselves to criticizing naturalism, but also aimed their fire at Moore and his intuitionism. Against naturalism the objection was raised that if "good" is simply to be another word for maximum pleasure, say, the definition fails to capture the proper point of using the term "good": it has been left outside the definition and is lost. The proper point of the word "good" is to give expression to approval; just as to call something bad is to express our disapproval of it. Further, approval or disapproval involves a desire to influence others; in making a moral judgement, one's intention is to alter or reinforce the attitude espoused by the other. In essence, then, a moral judgement, correctly construed, is the expression of one's attitude to something, of one's feeling about it. Hence, it stands to reason that there can be no scientific grounding of morality. Strictly speaking, our moral judgements are not judgements at all; they are not cognitions but expressions of our emotionally-informed attitudes to things. But that contention is tantamount to a rejection of intuitionism, inasmuch as intuitionism also made the assumption that morality turns on knowledge. Indeed, the moral judgement to the effect that something is good rested on an intuitive identification of the quality 'good' inherent in things or actions. So intuitionism was equally lacking in any sense of the connection between moral judgements and our attitudes and emotions.

In sum, we can say that whatever may have been the differences between naturalism and intuitionism, they had one thing in common: they considered moral judgements to be determinative of the character of objects and actions, which is why they regarded moral judgements as being either true or false. Such judgements amount to knowledge. This claim, however, was now being called into question. In the course of the 1920s, first the one, then the other moral philosopher began to conceive of moral judgements as expressions of emotions and as a means of eliciting emotions. In his *Ethics and Language* (1945), the seminal work of the theory (also known as the emotive theory), and representing the second stage in the theoretical progression, C. L. Stevenson pulls the threads together. The book offers a comprehensive and detailed examination of ethical reasoning. The key question informing the position is whether a difference in attitudes between one person and another can be traced back to different assumptions about the empirical data. If it can, and if it is possible to investigate the empirical data and to correct the assumptions of one or both parties, the difference in attitudes would be at an end. Another argument in discussions about ethical issues takes the form of a demonstration to the effect that there is a contradiction inherent in the attitudes espoused by one's opponent. But if progress down those routes is not possible, the discussant must resort to trying to sway the other emotionally, if he is unwilling to let the difference in attitudes persist.

However, it was not long before that position, too, was opposed. For there was one thing, and a very important thing, of which the emotive theory failed to take account, namely, that it never occurs to us to call our approval or disapproval a moral judgement unless in approving or disapproving we invoke a general rule. There is more to making a moral judgement than merely declaring what we happen to like or dislike. The difference between "good" and "bad," "right" and "wrong," resides in the reasons motivating the choice of one or other of two mutually incompatible actions. The difference is a difference in argumentation and reasoning, with the reasons offered consisting primarily in an appeal to a general principle. To call an action good or bad is tantamount to asserting that it agrees or disagrees with certain standards of goodness or badness. The moral use of words like "good," "right," and "ought" is governed by fixed rules. The emotive theory is therefore incorrect in claiming that moral judgements are grounded in emotions. Emotions are merely concomitants.

This brings us to the third stage in British moral philosophy, which identifies the characteristic feature of moral statements as their prescriptiveness. The chief advocate of this position is R. M. Hare, in his book *The Language of Morals*. The term "good" is used to indicate what one ought to do, to guide decision. This it can only do, however, by reference to a universal rule, inasmuch as he who has to make the decision needs to recognize the rule that is relevant to the situation in which he finds himself and which he must follow if his action is not going to be arbitrary. Granted, this applies to all instructions and prescriptions. What is distinctive about the ethical kind, however, is that the rules invoked are universal in the strict sense; one must be prepared to apply them anywhere and everywhere, and in respect of anyone and everyone.

Can morality, on this conception, be scientifically grounded? Indeed, it cannot. It is highly conceivable that there are a number of moral principles, all of them equally strong, and each of them individually a supreme principle not, in its turn, derivable from any higher principle. The choice between them cannot therefore be made by appeal to some general rule; rather, in each case the agent has to work out what the consequences would be, eliminate those principles which it is psychologically impossible for him to endorse, and from among the remainder select the principle that appeals to him most. There can be no distinguishing between true and false principles. All that is required is consistency. In other words, it is impossible to ground morality scientifically since in morality and science, respectively, we have to do with two different functions of language: in science with the language of assertion, which answers the question that asks for the facts, and in morality with the language of prescription, which answers the question that asks what we should do.

That does not mean, however, that individual moral propositions and rules cannot stand in logical relationships with one another. For prescription requires that the moral proposition contain a description of the state of affairs whose realization is prescribed, and the relationship between the descriptions that the one or the other moral proposition contains may very well be logical in nature. They may be incompatible, with the two states of affairs described not being co-realizable at one and the same time, or the one may be a consequence of the other.

Obviously, the ongoing debate in moral philosophy did not proceed in isolation from other, concurrent developments in the philosophical world during those years. This becomes particularly clear when we reach the fourth stage, whose defining work is P. H. Nowell-Smith's *Ethics* of 1954. The influence of the later Wittgenstein is manifest. The lesson learned from him was that language is used in many ways, and that words are not labels that we attach to things but tools which we use to do things. Consequently, to operate with dichotomies such as Stevenson's between descriptive and emotive language, or Hare's between descriptive and prescriptive, with the moral use of language reduced to the second in each category pair, that is, the emotive or the prescriptive, is all too generic an approach. The conception that we are examining here, then, is informed by a readiness to respect everyday usage.

When it comes to the question of whether morality can be scientifically grounded, the position sketched out above is opposed to both extremes. It is opposed to the standpoint represented by naturalism, which held that the strict logical derivation of moral propositions from established facts was possible. And it is opposed to the point of view that absolutely refuses to recognize the existence of moral knowledge, disputing the claim that an agent is capable of offering reasons for why he acts as he does—a standpoint that logical positivists and existentialists have also occasionally espoused. In contrast to these two extreme standpoints, the ordinary language theory asserts that the question is not that of whether or not some purported chasm separating sentences stating that something is good and sentences stating facts is bridgeable. Everything we say in daily life is determined by the contexts in which it is said, and those contexts contribute quite substantially to the determination of the meaning of the words. Since factual assertions are made in specific contexts, the intrinsic point of those assertions is to supply grounds for a sentence in which something is designated as good. Factual assertions were ever practical, just as sentences to the effect that something is good are not merely the expression of my own personal approbation but also the expression of the fact that my approbation is not unusual and that I am able to offer reasons for it. One should not, then, take a sentence detached from its context and ask what it means. One should ask: what are the contextual implications of its use in this instance, and what, when we hear and understand the sentence, would it be too bizarre to ask?

On the path traced by British moral philosophy in the twentieth century, which began with a revolt against naturalism, four milestones, as it were, may be set: moral propositions are understood to be rooted in intuition; they are subsequently regarded as the expression of an emotional reaction and a means of influencing emotions; thereafter their decisive feature is identified as that of prescribing and guiding choice, until ultimately, ordinary language gains ground and differentiates the whole.

At the close of his monograph, Blegvad very reasonably poses the question: What, finally, came out of it all? And candidly replies: Not terribly much! "Recent years have seen a growing appreciation of the fact that, by one-sidedly discussing what 'good', 'right', 'duty' and certain other words mean, moral philosophy has ended up in a blind alley" (*Den naturalistiske fejlslutning,* 199). Many have come to doubt the fruitfulness of the semantic method, and Blegvad himself is of their number. He asks, therefore, whether moral philosophy ought not rather to advance by tracing other routes and by embarking upon an investigation of the structure of the world of our experience, finding out how people experience the world in which they employ a moral vocabulary. Finally, to bring together the starting point in Moore and the end-point represented by Nowell-Smith: what Moore wanted was not simply to understand how we standardly use the word "good." It is not the conventional use of the word "good" that he is at pains to investigate. What he is after, rather, is the property the word stands for, the quality it denotes. Moore operates, then, with a disjunction: one can either set about investigating the ordinary use that is made of a word, or one can concentrate on what the word refers to and stands for.

In a sense it might be said that it is to the former enterprise that British moral philosophers apply themselves in the period that followed. They apply themselves ever more strenuously to the investigation of the use of language, addressing the task ever more acutely and, in consequence, becoming increasingly aware of the variety of different ways in which language is used, until this entire tendency informing research reaches its culmination in Nowell-Smith. That they embark upon this path and depart from Moore is, among other things, the result of their realization, stimulated not least by Wittgenstein, that Moore's conception of language—at the time of writing *Principia Ethica*—was far too crude. Moore assumed that words were like labels we attach to things—that the word "good" stood unequivocally for a corresponding property or quality.

This prompts the question whether there are but two options: either to follow the Moore of the *Principia Ethica* in assuming that the function of words is to designate items and then examine the objects and qualities thus designated, or with Nowell-Smith to assume that words are tools with which we do things, and then study language use. Is there not a third possibility, consisting in the assumption that language itself—not least in virtue of the words we use in ethical contexts—construes and interprets the world, its furniture and our own lives, so that the task becomes that of accounting for how they appear in our construal and reading of them? Is not this the task that Paul Diderichsen (in his article "Sprog og livssyn" [Language and View of Life] in *Livsanskuelsernes brydning i vor tid* [The Conflict between Outlooks on Life in Our Time] [Copenhagen, 1958]) reproaches moral philosophers with neglecting when he says that they have never raised the question as to how the world in which our ethical vocabulary operates is constituted? And is it not this fresh tack that Blegvad, in conclusion, suggests that we give a chance?

The exaggeration of the role of principles in ethical argumentation

As noted above, the role played by rules or principles is a far more modest one than that accorded to them in the third (and fourth) stage of British moral philosophy, where the relevant principles are thought to be either general, as in Stephen Toulmin, or universal, as in R. M. Hare. These two conceptions will now be examined in turn.

According to Toulmin, ethical reasoning takes, for instance, the following form: "I ought to give John his book back because I promised to let him have it back before noon." If a friend hearing me say this asks, "But do you really have to?" it may prompt me to offer a further reason: "Yes, I must because I promised to let him have it back." If the friend objects, "That makes no odds," I can move to a more general reflection still: "Yes, I ought to do whatever I promise anyone that I will." And if that principle is called into question, I can proceed to the most general and thus concluding argument: "Anyone who makes a promise is morally bound to keep it." There is nowhere to go beyond an appeal to an accepted social practice of this kind (Stephen Toulmin, *The Place of Reason in Ethics* [Cambridge, 1953], 146). The action that a situation enjoins, then, receives ethical weight in virtue of agreeing with a general principle. Thus far Toulmin.

But is that argumentation ethical? Is it not rather unethical? I would claim that it is. What happens in the process of generalization is that morality comes to exist for its own sake. In other words, it becomes moralism, which is morality's way of being immoral.

Is there, then, an alternative to generalization? There is indeed. Ethical reasoning can proceed down either of two distinct and opposed routes. It may, as we have seen, go the way of generalization: one can be prompted by an objection to defend one's decision by appeal to a more general consideration, and in so doing move further and further away from moral experience of a concrete kind.

The other route open to ethical reasoning proceeds via what might be called an explication of moral experience or an interpretation of the moral situation, a route distinguished by the fact that one stays with the concrete experience. So the answer to the friend's querying of the necessity of returning the book by noon might be: "But John needs the book." Should the friend object that John is surely able to find something else to read, I might, for instance, respond: "But John is planning on reading it this afternoon." If my friend persists and says, "That's surely to give too much consideration to John," I still need not strike the path of generalization but, staying with the explication of the actual situation, I may for instance say, "John trusts me and I would not want to risk losing that trust." In other words the argument appeals to the fulfillment of the lives of John and myself in and through our communication or interdependence.

It stands to reason that in an argumentation which consists of an explication of the actual ethical situation, we are much closer to the ethical phenomenon itself than we are in an argument that consists in generalization. Consequently, we do not reason in daily life by appeal to generalization, we do so only in philosophy. The conversation that Toulmin rehearses would never take place in everyday life but only in the Common Room of an English university, in some discussion of a lecture delivered before the university's philosophical debating society. But Toulmin imagines that that is how we discuss matters in ordinary life, too, and does not stop to consider that a man who in everyday life argued in the manner envisaged by Toulmin in his philosophical treatise is someone whom we would call a prig, a pedant. What a dreadful fellow he is, then, that Toulmin presents us with. He cares not two pins about John but is merely concerned with his own fidelity to his promises so that the social order may be preserved. This is the danger with philosophers constructing their own examples.

The overrating of the role of general principles and generalization in ethics is linked to a failure to distinguish between phenomenological description and an investigation of logical entailments. But the two inquiries must be kept separate, and at two points: in what concerns ethical action and in what concerns ethical reasoning.

The phenomenological description of the moral action is one thing; the investigation of what must be (logically) implied by an action in order for it to count as moral, is another. Those moral philosophers who hold that in a great many cases, to be moral, an action must be shown to fall under a general principle, must guard against insinuating reference to general principles into the phenomenological description. For with that, all spontaneity is excluded from morality, and the phenomenological description comes out as false in that the moral action in question certainly need not involve any reflection on a general moral principle.

But not only that. For when it comes to the reasoning, we must also distinguish between a phenomenological description of it and an investigation of what its logical entailments must be for it to count as ethical. The moral philosophers who hold that to qualify as ethical, an argument must imply a reference to a general principle, must therefore also here be careful not to suggest that moral argument must consist in making its purely logical derivation from a general principle explicit. At all events, it is not necessary. As we have observed, ethical argument may equally well, if not more appropriately, consist in an appeal to the concrete circumstances of a situation and an exploration of them. Ethical argument is one thing, the philosophical investigation of the argument's logical entailments is another, and it does not do to configure moral argument in the image of that philosophical investigation.

It is not only philosophically important to keep separate the two philosophical inquiries—the phenomenological description and the investigation of logical entailments—but also morally important. If we fail to do so, what we get is moralism, not morality. If we believe that part of moral experience consists in reflection on a general principle, and believe further that moral reasoning includes the appeal to a general principle that is logically implied by experience and reasoning, both the experience and the reasoning become moralistic. Whether or not Toulmin is correct in thinking that it is a moral act to return the book to John at the promised time because so doing is logically implied by the general principle that agents should keep their promises, one thing is certain: if the motivating reason for my returning the book to John at the promised time is not one of consideration for John but my resolve to live in accordance with the general principle that promises should be kept, my act is not moral but moralistic.

What function, then, has the general principle, or norm, in ethical argumentation? It has two functions. Since general principles, being grounded in very diverse forms of moral experience, are often variously justified, their purpose may be to get us to concentrate on where we agree and to deflect our attention from where we disagree. Irrespective of what, in the view of each of us, justifies the norm, and irrespective of the moral experiences on the basis of which we arrive at it, the important thing is that we agree upon accepting it. We content ourselves with that.

We also refer to the general norm when we cannot be bothered to go down into every detail in discussing a matter or lack the energy to explain our view. By appealing to a general principle, I procure ready ethical backing; I offer a purely provisional defence of the position I have adopted. To give an example: during the Second World War, individuals in the occupied countries joined the resistance on the basis of an appeal to the general principle that despots must be opposed by means of military force. Later, it became clear that the grounds and moral experiences motivating particular individuals to join the resistance were diverse in the extreme. Occasionally, those involved would actually find idiotic the reasons motivating the others.

The general principle, therefore, is but a conduit for thought; it is not decisive. It does not repose in its own self-evidence. On the contrary, its generality is a warning to us that we have reached only an intermediate point on the path of enlightenment.

But are we not bound to resort to moral principles every time we are in doubt as to the rightness of an action? And does not the doubt disappear when our moral code can be shown to contain a principle that is relevant to the action in question? It is not as simple as that, at least not always. It is not the case that the principles are already out there and that when doubt or mutual disagreement arise, all we have to do is to cast about for them. Rather, moral principles only come into being when occasioned by doubt and disagreement. But this means that there must be moral experience and understanding not constituted by principles but which must be translated into principles when doubt or disagreement prompt us to do so. And indeed there are. Before the relevant requirements on agency are requirements imposed by principles, they are requirements imposed by the specific and concrete situation, which latter enjoin us to act in ways answering to ethical predicates with descriptive content: by being courageous, patient, bold, forbearing, and so forth—including especially requirements prescribing communicative acts whose descriptions involve such predicates—a sovereign expression of life, the showing of trust, the offering of help, veracity, and the like. The correspondence is immediate, and the requirement of substantive conduct of some form or other imposed by the situation is not necessarily mediated by some moral principle. There exist expressions of life, which are already intrinsically moral or immoral—they do not become so only in virtue of principles.

The problem shifts if, instead of general principles, we operate with universal principles. R. M. Hare lays preponderant weight on the distinction between the general and the universal. The opposite of general is specific; the opposite of universal is singular. In contrast to that between universal and singular, the difference obtaining between general and specific is a difference of degree. "One ought never to make false statements" is a more general principle, says Hare, than "One ought never to make false statements to one's wife," but they are both universal principles, the latter equally so, for it says that "*no one* who is married should make false statements to his wife." Hare goes on to say that the principles to which one subscribes in moral judgement are rarely very general. But to qualify as moral, a moral judgement must always be transformable into a universal principle. If a judgement cannot be universalized, it is not moral. I cannot, in a particular situation, assert that my action is moral and bind myself to its performance without prescribing that anyone else in the same or a similar situation should do the same. But the universal principle may very well contain the most detailed specification of the situation; indeed, as far as that goes, all the features of the specific case may be represented in the universal principle. As we grow older our moral principles become more and more specific, often too complicated to admit of formulation (R. M. Hare, *Freedom and Reason* [Oxford, 1963], 38ff., 47–48).

To make it absolutely clear what Hare means, let us venture an objection. No matter how much two situations resemble each other, it is always possible to go into the degree of detail that will enable us to identify the difference between them. Consequently, provided that the description of a situation is sufficiently rich in detail, it will always be possible to ensure that the universal principle that one extracts from the act that one holds a particular situation to enjoin will not apply to even one other situation. But does that not mean that the universal principle is unusable? If it is to be of any use, is it not necessary to curtail the specification of the situation one seeks to universalize at an early enough point to ensure that the universal principle extracted may be applicable to other situations? In other words, does one not have to characterize a situation in a generalizing way, which is to say, accentuating certain features and abrogating others, if the universal principle extracted from that characterization is to apply to even one other situation? In a word, is it not, after all, the generality of a principle that renders it usable?

Hare disputes this. The universal principle is not rendered unusable through its not being applicable to even one other situation. For it to be usable, all that is required is that roles are reversed in one and the same situation. A debtor-creditor situation can be portrayed in such a wealth of detail that it must be regarded as unique, but I am still able to formulate a universal principle on the basis of the action which I hold this unique situation to enjoin, since nothing is needed for that beyond the fact that I, who am the creditor, imagine myself in the debtor's stead (ibid., 107).

But this implies that the usability of a moral principle consists of two things. One thing is guidance as to what the right action consists in, and depends on situations being alike. That is where the usability of the general principle lies. It is something else to use the moral principle in a role reversal exercise in order to determine whether I am making an exception of myself and thereby forgoing the possibility of justifying my action morally. That is where the usability of the universal principle lies. Since the test of the morality of one's own position, which is the point of universalizability, consists in role reversal, the success of the test will depend on the imagination of the individual. Is he capable of thinking himself into the position of the other? However that may be, the two species of usability must be kept separate. It will not do to require of the universal principle the usability of the general principle and require that the universal principle should be able to guide us in situations that are similar.

I shall now proceed to assess Hare's view, and let me say at the outset that I fail to see that substituting universality for generality gives moral principles any loftier a role in ethical argumentation. The supreme importance that Hare, like Kant, accords to the test determining the morality of an action, by examining whether a universal prescription is extractable from it, leads to preposterous results. Hare's example concerns a debtor-creditor situation that involves three individuals, and according to which A is in debt to B and B is in debt to C. Now Hare envisages B's maintaining that he ought to put his debtor A in prison while not consenting to being put in prison by C. B refuses to universalize his action, and hence Hare draws the conclusion that there exists no moral disagreement between B and a person, such as Hare, let us say, who does recognize the universalizability test, and is therefore not of the opinion that B should put his debtor in prison while not accepting being put in prison himself by his unpaid creditor. Despite B's and Hare's views being contraries, there is no moral disagreement between them, Hare contends, since one of the parties, B, does not recognize the universalizability test. All Hare can require of his opponent is his acknowledgement that he cannot offer a moral justification of his action (ibid., 98f.). But surely it is to accord exaggerated importance to the universalizability test to claim that, just because it goes unrecognized by an individual, there is no moral disagreement between the person who finds it acceptable to put his debtor in prison without finding it acceptable that he himself be put in prison by his creditor—and a person who refrains from putting his debtor in prison because he cannot accept his creditor's putting him in prison. But it is consistent for all that, as we shall see.

For Hare's claim—that there exists no moral disagreement because his opponent does not use the universalizability test—to be tenable, it cannot be a moral precept that the universalizability test be applied. But that is exactly what Hare, prior to offering his debtor-creditor example, argues. To be a moral principle, a principle must be universal. But the universalizability test through which we arrive at moral and universal principles is, note, not moral but only logical. If an agent thus refuses to apply the universalizability test and admits that he would never contemplate offering a moral justification of his position, then there is no moral disagreement. In other words, it is not a moral precept that people should be moral.

What is right in Hare's account is trivial, what is not trivial is wrong—on this head, for otherwise Hare's analyses are original and acute. It is true that if a person does not seek to give a moral justification of his actions, it is difficult to engage him in a discussion about moral issues; but that is a trivial observation. It is likewise true that if a person rejects the universalizability test, arguments that appeal to it will make no impression on him, and that is an even more trivial observation. But that moral disagreement should not obtain because one of the parties fails to recognize that form of moral argument is surely wrong—an exaggeration of the importance of moral argument to morality. This shows how fatal it is to stop at moral principles, even if they are universal, without going back to the ethically descriptive expressions of life in which those principles are grounded. Moral argument and its associated universalizability test come to constitute morality and immorality—as if morality and immorality were not prior.

It is no accident, then, that the fact that the universalizability test is logical and not moral is so important to Hare. It cannot be moral because it is that by which morality is first constituted. Only through the recognition of the universalizability test does one enter the realm of morality and immorality; if one fails to recognize it, one remains on the outside, since the precept enjoining one to subject oneself to the universalizability test is not moral. Nor is one in moral disagreement with the individual who recognizes the universalizability test. By contrast, if there are expressions of life which are moral and are that to which, when doubt and disagreement as to what is moral and immoral occasion it, the principles that formulate their content are traced back, then the same holds for the universalizability test, too. It is founded upon and formalizes the fact that, in their interdependence, our lives are fulfilled when we engage ourselves in the concerns of others and are subverted when we are solely preoccupied with our own affairs. There is therefore moral disparity between actions, the universalizability test notwithstanding. To have one's debtor thrown into prison is an iniquitous deed already, in virtue of its subversion of what, in their interdependence, our lives are intended to be. It does not become immoral merely in virtue of one's failing to find it acceptable that one's unpaid creditor has oneself put in prison. And by the same token, it is already a good action, by virtue of fulfilling the interdependence of our lives, to refrain from having one's debtor put in prison. It does not only become so through one's finding it unacceptable that one's real or imaginary creditor put one in prison. There exists already a moral disagreement between the person who has his debtor put in prison and the person who does not.

But there is a further objection to the claim that the universalizability test should be constitutive of morality. For the universalizability test may equally well provide the warrant for an immoral principle. Hare is fully aware of this. One might very well go in for one's debtor's going to prison as one would for oneself, qua debtor, by making appeal to the necessity of life's being a struggle in order that the world may be improved. And this is not merely an example invented by Hare. In pointing out that adversity and hardship are necessary for the mobilization of inner resources, a proponent of a typically reactionary attack on social services and the welfare state deems himself to be fully in line with the universalizability test since he is himself convinced that should he be crushed in the struggle for existence, he would take it like a man.

The nature of Hare's response to the individual who defends the struggle for existence as a moral principle is indeed indicative of his position. We can begin, he says, by contesting the idea that struggling to survive makes the world a better place to live. But if our opponent finds it admirable that the law of the jungle should reign and the world be comprised of supermen, we have to abandon that line of attack since our opponent is in accord with the universalizability test. Instead, we can try to convince him that he lacks the imagination to envisage what it would be like to suffer defeat in the struggle to survive. But if he maintains that, were he to be crushed, he would accept his fate, there is nothing we can answer him. He is a fanatic (ibid., 105f.). The option of entering into a discussion with him about what the fulfillment of our lives in their interdependence consists in and what it does not, and of contesting that it should consist in outdoing others, lies beyond Hare's horizon. If our opponent invokes the universalizability test, we must give up.

But how is it that Hare is able to regard a principle's universality as decisive for its moral status, when the opponent's immoral principle is just as universal? He can do so because he sees his opponent as being in a kind of perverse accord with the universalizability test—perverse because the opponent lacks imagination and is a fanatic. The opponent uses his lack of imagination and his fanaticism to evade the universalizability test while appearing to conform to it. To this we may reply that in order to know which principles are genuine and which are perverse, Hare must know what morality and immorality are independently of the universalizability test.

But why will Hare not admit to knowing this? Because he thinks that by so doing he would be unable to preserve ethics as a purely formal investigation of the logical properties of our moral vocabulary, separate from the advocacy of substantive views. But the cost of this restriction is that a large part of ethical argumentation eludes philosophical analysis. For, plainly, there is ethical argumentation that cannot be analyzed without our getting involved in discussion about it. If substantive moral views are to be kept out of ethics, construed as philosophical analysis—if, in other words, the aim is to maintain the distinction between ethics and meta-ethics, between philosopher and preacher—we shall not get to analyze the most important ethical argumentation.

Situation ethics

What has come to be known as situation ethics emerged as a reaction against the all too dominant role accorded to rules and principles in morality. Unfortunately, the reaction has been guilty of an equally great oversimplification but in the opposite direction. When the situation ethicist asserts that the uniqueness of each situation is such that considerations applicable to one situation can never be transferred to another, he misses an important distinction.

No past action can be performed anew; none of its consequences can be expunged, for the time in which we live will never return. The irrevocability of the act and the irreparability of the consequences that result from the irreversibility of time render the situation singular and give decision its ethical weight.

This does not prevent a situation occurring ten years ago from repeating itself, or people from repeatedly finding themselves in the same situations. Such recurrences do not detract from the situation's singularity since its singularity is a consequence of the irreversibility of time, and does not consist in a situation's invariably being unique in respect of its content.

We need to distinguish, then, between two things. One is the singularity of the situation, deriving from the irrevocability of the act, manifest in the irreparability of its consequences, and owed to the irreversibility of time; another is the question of the extent to which the situation is unique in respect of its content or of whether it has typical features. In most situations, typical features preponderate. Material ethical considerations are therefore in order. However, this does not mean that they must at all costs involve reflection on a principle.

In other words, from an ethical point of view, a situation is almost always at once both singular and typical. And there is nothing contradictory in that inasmuch as it is so in differing respects. It is singular with regard to the irreversibility of time, and typical in respect of its content. It is a fallacy, then, when the situation ethicist argues as follows: Since each ethical situation is singular, we can know nothing in advance about what our decision should be and a material ethics is impossible.[6]

Two types of evaluation

Twentieth-century British moral philosophy began, as noted above, with G. E. Moore's comparison of the property 'good' with the property 'red'. In two respects the properties are similar: neither is compound and neither can be analyzed. Only in an immediate and direct way, in an intuitive way, are we acquainted and familiar with them.

The deficiency in Moore's conception was his failure to distinguish between observation and interpretation. This is why he is unable to account for the difference between the experience of red and of good, respectively. Of course, he knows that the difference is fundamental, and indeed says that while redness is a natural quality, goodness is a nonnatural quality. But that is certainly not a solution to the problem—it is merely, at best, a formulation of it. Nor is it a very felicitous formulation, since it suggests the fallacy that the difference between the observation of red and the experience of good is a difference between two types of perception.

But this apart, it led to subsequent British moral philosophy's preoccupying itself almost exclusively with ethical predicates rather than with the phenomena themselves. 'Red' is a quality inhering in postboxes in Denmark, 'good' is a quality inhering in mildness; that was how Moore saw it. The step that should have been taken, but was not, is the step that leads back from the difference between red and good to the difference between the postbox and mildness, because it is that which is primary.

The narrowness characteristic of the development of British moral philosophy in the present century does not derive solely from the perpetuation of Moore's entrenched focus on the anatomy of ethical predicates, but derives also from the fact that Moore's study of ethically descriptive terms in the final chapter of *Principia Ethica* was not taken forward. If one is to believe British moral philosophy after Moore, then the ethical manifests itself primarily in the specific evaluative terms "good," "bad," "right," and "wrong". For it is they, together with the so-called deontological terms such as "duty" and "ought," which have provided the focus of inquiry. Over and over again, decade after decade, these six words have been analyzed, minutely and acutely, and to ever better effect. But all the substantive and descriptive modes of existence that are ethical in character—trust, distrust, veracity, mendacity, bravery, cowardice, cruelty, mildness, arrogance, mercy, and so on and so forth—have gone unexamined. Part of the explanation for Moore's applying himself to the examination of some of them has to do with the fact that he drew no distinction between ethics and meta-ethics. Subsequent philosophers cling to that distinction, which is why they dismiss his examination of ethical-descriptive phenomena as part of his personal idealism, having no bearing on philosophical ethics.

But by so doing they have committed themselves to the idea that ethics is evaluation and only evaluation. How often is the claim not heard that ethical sentences are not descriptive. But that is untrue. Many such sentences are indeed not descriptive, but there are many that are, as, for example, the sentence "Bertoald Lupigis is mild." This large division of ethical sentences, perhaps the most interesting, are ones British moral philosophy has cut itself off from in order to confine itself to what are clearly evaluations.

First, as we have seen, the inquiry focused on predicates rather than addressing phenomena, and second, in what concerned predicates, interest was focused exclusively on what were indisputably value words, thus giving rise to the undeniably narrow and possibly confused question: What is the difference between two sentences like "the postbox is red" and "mildness is a good thing"? What strikes me as a much broader and more interesting issue is that delivered by a comparison of the two sentences "the postbox is red" and "Bertoald Lupigis is mild."

What typifies ethically descriptive phenomena? Certainly, they force us to talk about evaluations in two very different senses. They present us, not with phenomena describable in a value-indifferent mode, which only later become the object of an evaluation (on an intuitive understanding of evaluation), but with phenomena that cannot be described in isolation from their goodness or badness. The conception of them as good or bad cannot be detached from their descriptions (unless the description is scientific, not phenomenological).

In the first case—when the phenomenon is describable in value-indifferent terms—it is I who produce the evaluation. A kind of sovereignty devolves on me. Not so that I can make the evaluation entirely as I please. I cannot approach it in an arbitrary manner. But the value of the phenomenon rests either on criteria and standards, on rules and precepts, or else on some end to which it is a means. My sovereignty of judgement consists in my bringing the phenomenon into the light of the purpose I intend it to serve or the criteria I apply to it. Out of that light, it may be described in value-indifferent terms.

But when it comes to the phenomena that cannot be described in abstraction from their goodness or badness, my sovereignty, in appraising their goodness or badness, is disabled. Sovereignty devolves on the phenomenon. Take trust and distrust, for instance: the positivity of trust and the negativity of distrust are not some evaluative accretions of which trust and distrust are the subjects, but inhere in the phenomena themselves. Positivity and negativity, respectively, reside in the very meanings of these two words. It runs counter to the intrinsic nature of trust, and is contrary to the very meaning of the term, to evaluate trust as a negative phenomenon. Strictly speaking, we are precluded from conceiving of trust as something negative. We may, of course, appraise trust as a negative thing, but this can only come about through our applying a perspective to trust in which we discount what trust itself imparts to us, namely, that it is positive. This is not merely a theoretical possibility—it does happen that, despite its nature, we appraise trust negatively because in a particular situation it is dangerous. Trust can be exploited; and so in bringing up a child we have to caution him or her against a trusting attitude in certain sorts of circumstances. But that does not make trust a neutral phenomenon which we are free to conceive of positively or negatively. It is only possible to evaluate it negatively by flouting its positive nature. The same applies, of course, to a positive evaluation of distrust: it is possible only in spite of the negativity of distrust.

Whether such phenomena are positive or negative, good or bad, is not first determined in our evaluation of them; it is not first decided in our engaging with them. They make me their own before I make them my own. They have intimated to me what is good and bad before I consider the matter myself and evaluate it. This is the reason for calling the positive expressions of life sovereign. Granted, as already noted, I may, in a particular case, deem it right to promote that whose intrinsic negativity the expressions of life have led me to grasp, as in the case where I teach a child to show distrust.

We can regard an end as so important that in the light of it we must deem negative, qua means, a phenomenon good in itself, but this does not negate the intrinsic goodness of the phenomenon. Our evaluation can thus run counter to the phenomena's own determinations of themselves as good or bad, but it cannot cancel them out; nor can it render the phenomena in themselves ethically indifferent. And an ethics that is not to amount to an oversimplification must be able to accommodate both determinations—both the determination by the phenomena themselves of what is good or bad, which I have received from them, and the determination of good and bad which is the product of my judgement.

The correlate of evaulation is the scientific investigation of the phenomena, which, in respect of positivity and negativity, are neutral. Only in a scientific investigation do the phenomena become neutral. For scientific investigation can only get going by adopting a reduction strategy, and among the things that are thereby eliminated are positivity and negativity. But if we are not presented with phenomena other than those that scientific inquiry has subjected to a reduction (seen from the ethical perspective), it is clear that only an evaluative effort can make them ethical again.

To go a step further in determining the difference between those phenomena that can be described in value-indifferent terms and those that cannot, one might ask: to what authority do we appeal when we seek to show that a description is false and when we seek to show that an evaluation is false? In respect of descriptions, ultimately the phenomenon itself is the authority. We refer to the observation of the phenomenon if it is observable, or to an intuitive understanding if we are dealing, say, with a text. The phenomenon itself resists the application of any false description. In the case of the evaluation of a phenomenon describable in value-indifferent terms, it is, in virtue of its being so describable, ruled out that it should itself act as the tribunal that may be appealed to when an evaluation is false. The relevant tribunals here are criteria and standards, rules and prescriptions, or an end-means relation.

But that distinction between description and evaluation does not hold good for those phenomena which cannot be described in abstraction from their goodness or badness. From love itself I know that it is good and from hate that it is bad, and not from end-means reasoning or from criteria and standards, rules and prescriptions.

Noncognitivism in British moral philosophy recognized the appeal inherent in evaluation and moral judgement and in the use of the words "good" and "bad," "right" and "wrong." To begin with, the appeal was construed as simply springing from the intention to work upon the emotions; later it was understood in terms of a prescription of what, by reference to a general rule, the other or the person himself should do. But who is making the appeal and to whom is the appeal being made? I appeal to another self no matter whether that other self is another person or myself. Or else I am the one to whom appeal is made, whether the appeal comes from another person or from myself.

But the question this raises is whether an appeal or a prescription may not proceed from something other than a "self." I claim that it can and that it does. There is another kind of appeal and one much more elemental in character. It proceeds not from a "self" but from definitive and sovereign expressions of life such as trust, sincerity, fidelity, mercy, and so forth. Trust contains an appeal to us to realize it, no matter how much we may ignore that appeal on account of our disappointment, our being offended, our nursing a grievance, or whatever it might be. Distrust contains an appeal to us to eschew it, no matter how eager we may be to disavow the appeal and provide reasons for our distrust. But noncognitivism leaves this out of account, assuming the tacit axiom that an appeal can only proceed from a "self" and can only find expression in an evaluation and moral judgement. It omits to examine the expressions of life that make an appeal to us, and to which we apply the ethically descriptive names. An important area of ethics thus falls outside the purview of its inquiry.

But the peculiarity of these phenomena is that, notwithstanding that they exist only in our realization of them, they still have a claim on us. If the distinction I have argued for is rejected and it is argued that when love is considered good and hate bad it results from an evaluation that places these phenomena in the light of an end-means relation, or of criteria and standards, rules and prescriptions, the question arises as to the nature of the end or the criteria, standards, rules, and prescriptions that lead us to deem love good and hate bad. If we reply that the end, the standard, the criterion, the rule, the prescription are not in themselves good or bad, we are guilty of the naturalistic fallacy. If we declare that they are good in themselves, we make a superfluous move—we have gone back to the conception of love or some comparable phenomenon as something that is good in itself, and of hate or some comparable phenomenon as something that is bad in itself. A third possibility is to opt for Hare's and Kant's view, according to which a rule is ethical because it is prescriptive and universalizable, but that is not, as I have tried to show, a satisfactory answer.

Purely terminologically, it is arguably somewhat infelicitous to speak of evaluation not only in respect of the phenomenon that can be described in value-indifferent terms, but also in respect of that which is unamenable to description in isolation from its goodness or its badness. The relationship to the relevant descriptions is too disparate in the two cases for it to be felicitous to call both of them evaluations. Terminologically, the felicitous choice would arguably be to reserve the term evaluation for the evaluation which relies on criteria and standards, on rules and prescriptions, and on the end-means relation. But what the other should be called I must confess that I do not know.

Morality and the formation of ideals

Any investigation of ethically descriptive phenomena will surely uncover many categorial differences. Some of the phenomena, traditionally called virtues, are character traits acquirable through practice—courage is one such—while others are emotions, such as, say, pity, which Moore, incidentally, wrongly considers a virtue; and yet others again are sovereign expressions of life. But there is a difference that has implications for ethical argumentation. In respect of some ethically descriptive phenomena, we can well imagine that they will some day have lost their appeal, their names having lost their gerundive power. Indeed, we may have seen an instance of such a loss ourselves, not because the phenomenon in question has necessarily become a negative but rather, say, because it is now regarded as ludicrous. Let us take a somewhat droll example where, moreover, the cause of the change is obvious. Now that in the space of three years the standard of living has risen as much as it did in thirty years at the beginning of the century, combined with the circumstance that, given inflation, we have seen our debt shrink, perhaps several times, without our needing to service it, thrift, once a virtue, has become a rather ridiculous compulsion. Thus has the world moved forward—at least we do not consider it to have regressed on that account. Even if our attitudes have become too ingrained for us to change, we are still able to appreciate that others deem it progress that thrift has become mildly lunatic. By contrast, we cannot imagine an ethically descriptive phenomenon such as integrity losing its appeal and the term its gerundive power without the world being the poorer for it.

The difference between thrift and integrity is that thrift belongs to the realm of ideals while integrity belongs to morality, and that is a distinction which has implications for ethical argumentation. These latter might consist in our pointing it out to ourselves or to others that an ethically descriptive phenomenon which we assumed to belong to morality belonged, in fact, merely to the realm of ideals; and an even more important form of ethical inquiry consists in evaluating ethically descriptive phenomena that attach to ideals according to the scope they afford the ethically descriptive phenomena that belong to morality. One example is when sociologists and psychiatrists are critical of the idea of romantic love on the grounds that, by so elevating expectations that they are bound to be disappointed, it gives rise to infidelity. Romantic love, an ideal so characteristic of and potent in Western culture, is thus evaluated according to the scope it gives an ethically descriptive phenomenon like fidelity.

The distinction between ideals and morality is one I have taken from Hare, since I find his distinction important. Were we to adopt it, we would be in a position to discuss the articulation of ideals in a morally relaxed way, which is hardly ever the case today. Ideals are taken for morality, which results in people proclaiming their own standpoint and condemning that of the other, rather than engaging in a debate in which arguments are deployed that are the fruits of analysis. However, I shall not address that issue here but will restrict myself to saying that no matter how fruitful I find his distinction, I find Hare's own development of it somewhat wanting. Hare is content to rejoice in disagreements about ideals. Since my ideal does not inconvenience my neighbor, no matter how much it diverges from his, our disagreement harms neither human living together nor life in society. It is better that such divergences exist than that we should all live and think in conformity. The debate prompted by disagreement about ideals and the arguments in play there go unexamined by Hare. Is that simply because he has not yet had the time? Perhaps—but there may also be two other reasons.

One is that no analysis of a discussion of conflicting ideals, with an account of which arguments are convincing and which are not, could be undertaken without the philosopher asserting substantive moral viewpoints and thus abandoning his meta-ethical stance.

The second reason is that Hare, just like the other British philosophers, is not interested in ethically descriptive phenomena, and so neither is he interested in the implications yielded by his distinction between morality and ideals for the categorial division among the ethically descriptive phenomena that I have identified above.

More incisively, the difference between good, bad, right, and wrong on the one side, and diligent, upright, and courageous on the other, consists, Hare contends, in the fact that for the first group the prescriptive meaning of the terms is primary while the descriptive meaning is mutable; for the second group, by contrast, the descriptive meaning is fixed and the prescriptive meaning mutable. But I fail to see how that can be so. Indeed, there are ethically descriptive words, for instance, "honest" or "merciful," whose prescriptive meaning is just as fixed as "good" and "bad," "right" and "wrong," as against, say, "thrifty" and "diligent," whose prescriptive meaning is mutable. The difference between "good" and "bad," "right" and "wrong," and words such as" thrifty," "diligent," "upright," and "merciful" is, then, something else: it is, following Nowell-Smith, that as far as the first group goes, the act and the conduct prescribed possess descriptive features without the meanings of the words involving a characterization of what they are, while the descriptive meanings of the second group of words consists in a specification of those descriptive features. "Good" does indeed have a descriptive meaning, but it is dependent on context, in the absence of which its descriptive meaning is nil. The descriptive meaning of "upright," by contrast, is substantive, and can be explicated without reference to any context.

Notes

1. Notwithstanding the fact that in common parlance the word "mercy" is used primarily in religious contexts, I shall be using it here and elsewhere in a purely human sense. For two reasons. First, because there is no other word that renders its meaning. Aside from the term "helpfulness," all related words—"pity," "compassion," and the like—express a passive attitude to the person in distress, and "help-

fulness" is too broad; the recipient of help does not have to be in need and in distress. Second, although the word comes to us from Judaism and Christianity, it derives—if we think of Jesus' teaching—from what is universal in Christianity and not from what is specific to it. Its meaning is made vivid by the story of the Good Samaritan, a thoroughly human story, so human that it has in fact become a legal offence not to show the mercy shown by the Samaritan. The specifically religious import—that the mercy shown one is unmerited—is extraneous to the story. Consequently, we can disregard its religious import when using the word in ordinary human contexts.

2. It can hardly be doubted that the idea that what is radical is unmanageable is Christian in inspiration. It is equally certain that the radical element in Jesus' teaching is as manageable as anything. In fact it sometimes happens that the radical is defined as the most manageable of all that is manageable. That is no exaggeration when radicalness consists in passing the other a cup of water. In normal circumstances, and it is the normal case that is relevant, no great effort is required. There is no contemplation of abnormal circumstances in which, say, the thirsty individual is in a desert, so that reaching him requires enormous effort, or of his being in a concentration camp, so that getting to him involves putting one's life at risk.

One might also turn to a recurrent theme in Jesus' teaching, his polemic against the Pharisees, and ask after its thrust. Is he complaining that the Pharisees compromise the demand enjoined upon all? That they make it too easy for their compatriots, turning life into a manageable affair? No, the very opposite is the case; Jesus accuses the Pharisees of making it unmanageable.

It is equally clear that, in contrast to the Pharisees, Jesus does not go along with the idea that so long as people live conventionally respectable lives, all is well. He does not, in the name of conventional morality, relativize the requirements made of people. He maintains the radicalness of the Golden Rule but asks the Pharisees, as it were: Where on earth did you get the idea that the radical is the unmanageable?

3. Not to simplify matters unduly, it has to be added that there is also something positive involved in the fear of other people. There is a kind of intrusion into the life of the other that we recoil from. The other wants to be surrounded by, and to move within, a zone in which he is inviolable. We hold back from intruding into that sphere; the threat of embarrassment keeps us from doing so, no matter how completely we see through the other. At any rate, we need to be extremely angry to demolish his invisible wall.

The zone of inviolability that the individual lays claim to can vary greatly in extent. It can be so extensive that we neither can nor will respect it. It is at its most extensive when the individual covers everything that comes up with his conceit. But that it is a zone of inviolability is made clear, for example, by the fact that the conceited individual cannot bear to be the target of criticism. And when people respond to criticism with falsehoods which are palpably such, and which are completely beside the point and so inane that they deny the critic all judgement, it is again evidence that the person criticized feels threatened in his zone of inviolability. The latter is respected on this second head. If one has said what one wished to say, one does not pursue it but swallows the untruth and the fact that one's judgement has gone unacknowledged.

Conversely, the more objectivity and detachment a person brings to the matters in which he is involved, the smaller, or at least the less demanding for others, is his zone of inviolability. But it is always considerable in extent, even when not extreme.

4. Translators' note: The chapter to which Løgstrup refers is not included in the present volume.

5. Translators' note: The above extract is from Robert Musil, *The Man Without Qualities*, translated from the German by Eithne Wilkins and Ernst Kaiser (London: Secker & Warburg, 1960), vol. 1, *A Sort of Introduction. The Like of It Now Happens*, 71.

6. There are two further points to note concerning situation ethics. It does not distinguish between the ethico-political and the ethico-existential situation of choice. And it is incorrect in asserting that to be authentic and to enjoin a person's complete commitment, the decision must exclude understanding. I have treated both these points in *The Ethical Demand* and *Kunst og Etik* (Art and Ethics) and shall not enter into them here.

FOUR

Norms and Expressions of Life

Task and character

We are normally unaware of what it is that sustains us in our actions and enterprises. Initially, and for the most part, it is hidden, so preoccupied are we with the things we want to accomplish through our actions, so preoccupied are we with the goals and plans we have for our enterprises. Not until we experience a failure or a crisis do we realize what sustains us in our actions and enterprises. If something goes wrong, we become conscious of that which we should have been led by, but were not. When that which we had aimed to accomplish comes to nothing, even though the external obstacles were far from insurmountable, we are forced to admit that what let us down was our perseverance. The failure stirs up into consciousness our own weakness of character, and through the contrast made visible by this failure, we realize that what sustains us and fails us in the completion of our tasks is our character. To take an example: many begin academic studies without having learned to work thoroughly. Let us imagine such people attending a course on Kant's *Critique of Pure Reason*. They prepare well. They also find the thoughts in Kant's work intriguing, and lack neither diligence nor interest. Nevertheless, after a while they must concede they haven't the slightest idea of what it all means. Everything they have read and heard has been in vain, a waste of time. They must either give up or begin again. But they have no real choice, for they are too captivated by philosophy to let it go. They must therefore begin again on their own, determined not to leave a single sentence until they have understood it, no matter how long that takes. Not until reaching this stage—perhaps years into their studies—do they learn to work thoroughly. It took a *crisis* (although the word may seem a bit inflated) to make them conscious of the fact that what a person's work rests on is either thoroughness or superficiality.

Crisis having revealed either thoroughness or superficiality, either strength or weakness of character, it is equally important that these once again return to their hidden existence. What is decisive is that a person should work thoroughly not for the sake of thoroughness, but for the sake of *Critique of Pure Reason*. Personal character traits can certainly be trained, but not for their own sake, and not without an element of pleasure. Presumably very few people possess a natural proclivity to work thoroughly. Most require practice and training. From an educational and self-educational point of view it is important that character traits are not trained and developed by paying attention to them and worrying about them. If a character trait is to develop, one must shift one's attention away from it and focus on the task it is meant to benefit, and which may be impossible to complete without it. Continuing along the lines of our example, there is only one way to learn to work thoroughly, and that is to become sufficiently preoccupied with the task at hand. This alone intensifies both the satisfaction of having succeeded because one has worked thoroughly, and the dissatisfaction of having failed because one has worked superficially, and that is the essence of the character trait we call thoroughness.

Thus, there is an important difference. While we grapple with a task, we develop the character trait upon which its performance depends. This trait takes root because of the pleasure we experience at achieving a successful outcome, and even earlier as we struggle to overcome the obstacles. But the shift is fatal if one turns away from the task and focuses on the character trait in order to take pleasure in it. This very quickly becomes destructive, and in more ways than one. The character trait stiffens and becomes a caricature of itself, and one's self-satisfaction begins to swell. Something similar applies to discontent. It is one thing to feel dissatisfied after taking a superficial approach, but quite another to become immersed in one's own lack of character. The latter only makes one sink even deeper into it. When it comes to character—either one's own or someone else's—it can only be trained and developed by the prospect of taking pleasure in one's work, and by experiencing this pleasure. Nothing is gained by appealing to someone's character, or reproaching them for a lack of character.

The question we must now ask is: what reason are we to give for our enterprise and our actions? There are two possibilities, since all enterprise and all actions are partially called forth by goals we have set for ourselves and tasks that must be performed, and partially borne by character and motives. There can be no doubt that the goals and the tasks must supply the justification for what we do, and not our character or motives. This also applies when an ethical justification is required. This is because of something Kant saw clearly: that the same character trait can be used to serve both good and evil. Thoroughness is a prerequisite for understanding *Critique of Pure Reason,* and thoroughness is a prerequisite for committing a successful break-in. Carelessness will only lead to another Watergate scandal.

The hiddenness of the spontaneous expressions of life

Many factors besides character and lack of character underlie our enterprising lives, among them the spontaneous expressions of life such as trust, compassion, openness of speech, and hope, and also such concerns as envy, hate, jealousy, and vindictiveness, which are obsessive and revolve within us. It goes without saying that we are aware of the last type, for once we have become obsessed with them, they incessantly mill around in our consciousness, taking possession of it. The spontaneous expressions of life, however, are hidden; we are unaware of them. The reason for this is the same reason that explains why our character or lack of character mainly leads a hidden existence. We are far too preoccupied with the things we are doing and have to accomplish and see through to the end.

The same applies to the spontaneous expressions of life as applies to language. Language insists on being overlooked in favor of the topic. The spontaneous expressions of life insist on being overlooked in favor of the content with which the situation endows them. Trust insists on being overlooked in favor of whatever is at stake in the given situation, whether it be the other person's faithfulness, tenacity, resolve, or whatever it is one trusts in. Pity[1] insists on being overlooked in favor of the action that is best suited to alleviate the suffering of the other person in the given situation. In favor of the action to which the spontaneous expression of life spurs us on, the expression itself pulls back, unnoticed. In its latent presence the spontaneous expression of life does not distract us from that which the situation indicates should be done. Itself hidden, the spontaneous expression of life sets individuals free to do what it demands of them (see *Skabelse og Tilintetgørelse* [Creation and Annihilation], 88).

The conflict brings the expression of life out into the light of consciousness

It takes crisis, collision, and conflict for us to become aware of the expression of life. A person may experience the conflict that voicing one's opinion comes at a price. The price does not have to be very high for people to be tempted to keep their opinions to themselves. We do not wish to pay a price that consists in having the person we criticize drop us, so we refrain from voicing our criticisms. Such a conflict can give occasion to formulate that which is definitive in the spontaneity of speech, namely its openness. The formulation is marked by having been brought about by a conflict situation. It appears in a negative and restrictive form; it becomes a prohibition: You must not hide your opinion out of fear of other people, or your friends.

Conflicts come in all shapes and sizes; they can be harmless, and they can be terrifying. Let me take an extreme example that has occurred during our century often enough: the systematization within a society of people informing on one another. Such a conflict situation sheds a reflective light back upon what used to undergird people's actions. Preoccupied with the things upon which they agreed or disagreed, captivated by plans, whether they had the same thoughts or conflicting thoughts about them, at the time people never gave a thought to the fact that in everything we say and do, we trust one another. Openness turns out to be the hidden foundation of our actions. We realize this in the crisis situation, when the foundation is pulled out from under our feet. We do not discover it until it is gone.

Enmity crisis and foundation crisis

We must distinguish between what could be called an enmity crisis and a foundation crisis. Other names might also be applied to this distinction, but what I mean is the following: People can bicker and fight with one another, become furious at one another, one person can think the other is stubborn and uncooperative, and they can begin to battle one another, bitterly and obstinately. But even if it goes so far that people become each other's enemies, it is very possible that in this enmity the two parties know where they have each other. They are not playing an underhand game. This is an enmity crisis, not a foundation crisis.

A foundation crisis, on the other hand, exists when it is part of one's view and approach to act under false pretences, deceiving the other person. One cannot trust anything said or done by people who are partners in collusion. Not only are their words untrustworthy, but the very openness that is constitutive of all speech has been rendered untrustworthy.

The unpleasant thing about the foundation crisis is that it cannot be made to result in enmity. That is the paradox of it. The reason, however, is obvious. If we find ourselves in a foundation crisis, only one thing can clear the air, and that is taking the embarrassment of open conflict upon ourselves. But this is precisely what such people will not do, for if they did, it would be revealed that the untrustworthiness is incorporated into their view and approach. Their policy stands and falls with the foundation crisis, and therefore every enmity crisis must be avoided.

The spontaneous expressions of life defy justification

Character and the spontaneous expressions of life are similar in the sense that they undergird and guide our actions in life, doing so in a way that remains hidden until we encounter dereliction and failure, conflict and collision. But there are two differences, as I have already mentioned.

One difference is that character exists to perform tasks, and that it is developed during the performance of these tasks. The spontaneous expressions of life exist to allow our coexistence and communal life to endure and develop. They are summoned forth by the very coexistence and communal life that they realize.

Another difference is that character can be used to perform both agreeable and disagreeable tasks, whereas the spontaneous expressions of life as such are ethical. They have a definitive content that can be described—although it cannot be described value-indifferently, any more than it can be described while abstracting from the impulse issuing from a given expression's definitive content. This is because the spontaneous expressions of life are unconditional.

This unconditionality manifests itself in the fact that as soon as an expression of life is called upon to serve another purpose than its own, it disappears or is transformed into its own opposite. It is through this disappearance or distortion that we can empirically establish the quality of unconditionality. This unconditionality consists in defying any ulterior motive. Mercy consists in an impulse to free another person from their suffering. If it serves another purpose, such as stabilizing society, it is replaced by indifference towards the other person's suffering. The ulterior motive transforms mercy into its own opposite.

This is why the spontaneous expressions of life defy all justification. The very moment we seek to give a reason for them, we make them contingent upon that which we present as our reason, and they become corrupted right then and there. We have made them a means to obtain a goal other than their own: a means for the goal that is present in the justification.

But should we not justify why distrust is preferable to trust, hate to love, lies to truth?[2] No, these are not genuine questions. They do not arise out of a predicament we find ourselves in; they do not arise out of experience. The questions are humbug. The only answer is that if distrust is preferable to trust, hate to love, lies to truth, then coexistence and communal life cease. We can undermine the expressions of life, and we do, but not without life being destroyed. If trust, openness, compassion between us vanished and no longer broke through our attempts to destroy them, we would be done for. In this lack of any other answer, we see the spontaneous expressions of life defy justification.

To sum up: the spontaneous expressions of life lead a hidden existence. It takes crisis situations, colliding duties, and conflicts to stir them up into consciousness so that we can engage in putting them into words. The formulations of the spontaneous expressions of life, occasioned by crises, collisions, and conflicts, are ethical norms.

Norms and expressions of life

One might ask which comes first, the norm or the spontaneous expression of life. There are those who claim the norm comes first, so that the characteristic, definitive nature of the spontaneous expression of life is an inward integration, a profound incorporation of the norm—an "internalization," as it is called these days. I believe the opposite, that what comes first is the spontaneous expression of life, and that the norm is a formulation of it occasioned by the fact that the spontaneous expression of life, with its definitive nature, has run into a crisis. Supporting my view is the virtually unlimited number of variations in which one and the same norm can be formulated. We can put it into words in the most different ways, just as the norm can take all manner of degrees, ranging from the specific to the general, from the concrete to the abstract. The more closely we stick to the crisis situation, the colliding duties, the conflicts that give us occasion to become conscious of the spontaneous expression of life and put its particular nature into words, the more concrete and specific the norm becomes. The more we enter into boundless speculation, the more abstract and general the formulation of the norm. The wording could be: Do not let fear of forfeiting a chance to be admired make you hold back or disguise your opinion. Or the wording could be: Do not let fear of your friend make you go along with what he or she says, although you believe your friend is in the wrong. Or the wording could be: Refrain from lying.

An ethical norm does not become fundamental because it is general or abstract, but because it is founded in a spontaneous expression of life—which applies no less to a concrete and specific norm than it does to an abstract and general norm.

It goes without saying that just as the spontaneous expression of life defies justification, so does the fundamental ethical norm, and for the same reasons. But one is only aware of this if one considers the norm as founded in the expression of life. If, on the other hand, one considers the norm to be the primary element, the justification leads nowhere—a point to which I will return later.

The unconditionality of the expression of life and the norm's "ought"

Quite often, what becomes of our charity is nothing more than an ineffectual impulse. The mutual dependence—the interdependency—does not disappear, however, and it makes itself felt as a reminder that we live at the expense of others, indifferent to their suffering. The mercy we have betrayed is stirred up into consciousness. The acts that mercy would have done, but which never came to pass, become acts that ought to be done. They become our duty.

In other words, it is the empirically establishable unconditionality of the sovereign expression of life that our betrayal transforms into the "ought" of the norm. This "ought" is rooted in and springs from the unconditionality of the expression of life.

The problem for moral philosophy is: Where does the norm's "ought" come from? In what or in whom is the norm's "ought" rooted? My answer is: Important norms are rooted in expressions of life such as trust, the openness of speech, mercy. Two things can be said of these expressions of life: they are—preferably—latent, and they are unconditional.

The action's conditionality

Neither the unconditionality of the expression of life nor the "ought" of the norm renders reflection and argument superfluous. The expression of life gives rise to actions, and just as unconditional as the expression of life is, so conditional on the given situation and circumstances are the actions to which it gives rise. And just as conditional as the action is on the situation and its circumstances, so numerous will the reflections and arguments required in the given situation be for anyone seeking to determine the right action. In one situation the right course of action is obvious, in another it is almost impossible to determine, and in between lie a wide range of situations that are more or less clear.

When we have to choose between one action and another, one norm and another, it becomes especially clear that we are in a situation that leaves us with several options while at the same time limiting them to a few. The second aspect is just as important as the first, for it demonstrates that the potentially relevant actions are always conditional upon the situation and its circumstances. Each of the possible actions consists in taking a stand on certain circumstances connected with the situation: accepting them or doing what one can to change them. The conditionality of the action sets in motion reflections that consist in weighing the arguments against one another: the arguments for accepting the circumstances and the arguments for changing them in one way or another. The question is what will happen as a result of the options upon which we choose to act. When the choice is moral, one norm stands against another—which by no means always implies that the choice can be made by prioritizing the norms. Quite often the weighing-up has to do with how large the risks are of really running into the potential disadvantages or misfortunes occasioned by one action or the other, or with how large the chances are of really achieving the prospective advantages offered by one action or the other. Naturally, motives also play a role. What tempts us is choosing the action that will allow everything to continue in the same old rut.

Yet there are also enough situations in which the only defensible thing to do is obvious. Sometimes reflection can even be not merely superfluous but actually inappropriate, as it only functions to divert one from doing what must be done. The action nevertheless remains conditional, even in those situations in which the right thing to do is obvious. Behavior and actions are never, ever, solely determined by the expression of life. This appears from the fact that people, when held accountable for their actions, can always argue in favor of them, and not only when the arguments have been stirred up into reflections for and against the actions because there was a conflict as to the right thing to do. The arguments were also present when the action was immediately obvious from a situation in which what ought to be done was apparent, only they were latently present because they were superfluous. As immediate, as spontaneous as an action may be, that does not make it any less rational. Rationality is brought forth when the request for accountability is made. In short, by virtue of the action's conditionality the arguments are present, hidden or manifest, conscious or unconscious.

Then again, this also means that when someone is held accountable for their actions, the arguments can only consist in a reference to the actions' conditionality upon the situation and its circumstances. It is out of the question to invoke the expression of life, even though it may have undergirded the action. We must accept that an expression of life never realizes itself without a situation; people will always find themselves in a situation where the circumstances condition the action in which the expression of life realizes itself.

The relationship between expression of life and action is not one of application. The expression of life does not let itself be applied to the behavior any more than the behavior allows itself to be subsumed under the expression of life as an instance of it. The behavior is sustained by and rests in the expression of life. The expression of life does not determine the behavior or dictate the action, and it does not preclude rational reflection or judgement. On the contrary, it demands them.

So little does the expression of life determine the behavior that in certain cases the only appropriate thing to do is to suspend the expression of life.

Before briefly discussing this question I would like to expressly note that unconditionality and conditionality are not meant in the causal sense. It is possible to give a causal explanation of how the expression of life's unconditionality came about in the history of humankind and the individual. But that does not offset the fact that the expression of life, together with its content—which consists in precluding any ulterior motive—is unconditional. Also, the action's causal conditionality differs from the conditionality consisting in the action receiving its rational form from the situation and its circumstances.

Suspending the expression of life

In certain cases the conditionality of the action can make it necessary to suspend the expression of life. The only ethically defensible course can be to go against the openness of speech, to put the other person on the wrong track, namely, when the other harbors destructive intent and holds power. The expression of life can therefore be suspended, and it can be necessary, indeed a duty, to do so. In a dictatorship, being sincere when dealing with the secret police is inadmissible.

That is not to say that sincerity and insincerity are equivalent, and that we must find justification for sincerity being preferable to insincerity. What we must justify is our suspending sincerity. We must be able to account for our being in exceptional circumstances, and we justify this precisely by saying that we are dealing with an individual who harbors destructive intent, and that this individual holds power. Sincerity, however, defies justification. The suspension does not repeal it. It remains equally irreplaceable despite all. That is also why it returns straightaway, as soon as the extraordinary situation no longer exists.

Suspension of the sustaining expressions of life is not to be taken lightly and should only be resorted to as the last alternative. We must not imagine ourselves to be in exceptional circumstances as soon as things stop going exactly as we would like them to go. If we do, it will lead to the breakdown of all coexistence and communal life.

The problem of justification

The problem of justification is usually treated in a manner different from the one to which I have adhered above. We can embark on the discussion of this problem by stating the fact on which we can all agree: our actions in life are directed by norms that we either observe or violate. As already mentioned, the problem for moral philosophy is: Where does the norm's "ought" come from? On what or whom is the norm's "ought" based? In order to find an answer to this question, our thoughts can take one of two directions: upwards or downwards. They can, as has been the case above, move downwards to the expressions of life. This has the advantage of bringing one to the phenomena that give rise to the ethic that has always already arisen. These are the expressions of life along with the actions in life they sustain. But the direction one's thoughts take can also move upwards in a generalization or universalization of the norms, and that is what most often happens. One seeks for the ultimate principles, which in their capacity as ultimate are supposed to endow the norms with their validity. Over and above the norms, one seeks for a metanorm.

The path of generalization goes from the situation-based claim to the reasons for that claim, and in the reasons one goes further, seeking for synoptic theories and criteria. Yet no matter how far up the scale of generality one moves, one can continue to ask what it is that makes the general norm ethical. And finding no answer, one must settle for deciding in favor of the norm. In other words, the principle one ends up with when ascending in degrees of generality is characterized by two traits: it is underivable and it is all-encompassing. But no ethical validity arises from these two traits. What is lacking is the confrontation with an ultimate authority. And because this is lacking, one resorts to decision, despite the fact that in doing so one has truly given up the confrontation. Moral philosophy has ended in what is referred to as "decisionism."

In the process of generalization we have left the phenomena behind, for the two traits—being underivable and all-encompassing—are not traits of the phenomena but traits of claims. Instead of seeking the confrontation that only the concrete phenomenon can offer, one seeks it in the underivable[3] and encompassing qualities of the claim. These two traits are supposed to fill in for the confrontation but are unable to, and one concedes this by seeking refuge in decision.

Things are no better when one chooses the path of universalization. In that case what applies is this: As specific as the moral situation may be—even if it is so specific that it is unimaginable the situation should ever repeat itself—an action becomes morally good by virtue of the fact that anyone coming to be in the situation may be required to undertake it. In other words, morally good behavior is behavior that can be universalized. This means, however, that because it constitutes morality, the test of universalization is not itself a moral principle but a logical principle. From this it follows—and it is a consequence the British philosopher R. M. Hare draws with eyes wide open—that if a person will not recognize the logical principle, namely the universalization test, there is no moral disagreement between that person and the one who approves the universalization test. This is unreasonable, but not something I shall discuss further here since I have done so elsewhere (in *Norm og spontaneitet*, 40–44) [included in chapter 3 in this volume]. I would simply point out that this means that here, too, we enter the sphere of morality only by means of a decision. We must decide in favor of the universalization test if we wish to be within the realm of morality.

The essence of all this is that the decision to which one is referred, whether taking the generalizing or universalizing approach, as a sort of deliverance from the justification process, so to speak, is a replacement for the expression of life one began by disregarding. The decision is just as existential as the expression of life. That is why it can take the place of the expression of life. However, when serving as a surrogate for the expression of life, the decision suffers from two deficiencies. First, it is just as devoid of content as the expression of life is definitive in content, and second, it precludes confrontation, whereas the expression of life with its unconditionality offers such confrontation.

The question is: What provides a breeding ground for ethics; from what does it grow? There are two possible answers: Ethics grows from expressions of life, which are inherently ethical, and in such an elemental way that one does not even think of them as being ethical. Who thinks of the act of speaking as ethical? Yet all speech is ethical, thanks to its innate openness. The other possible answer to the question of what ethics arises from is: Ethics grows from norms. But this leads us astray from the very start. The form and wording the norm lends to the problem of justification is: Which norm is the highest? Which commandment in the law is the greatest? But this is not a question that has a specific occasion. It arises out of a philosophy that is self-sustaining, or it arises out of an attempt to get a systematic grip on a wildly multiplying casuistry.

If we give in to the tendency to limit ethics to norm and decision, we cause the expressions of life to fall outside the realm of ethics. Admittedly there is nothing to prevent us from advocating a narrow definition of ethics and claiming that ethics does not arise until we are in doubt about, or disagree about, the right thing to do. In this case the expressions of life become pre-ethical. What speaks in favor of such language is that it is in accordance with the immediate attitude that is taken aback at, or perhaps even resists, the notion that even speech is an ethical expression of life. And I can consent to the use of such language for that matter. However, I can only do so on one condition: that we remember that just as philosophy is incapable of pulling itself up by its bootstraps but is based on and grows from non-philosophy, so ethics is incapable of pulling itself up by its boot-straps but is based on and grows from pre-ethical expressions of life.

If I am to consent to this narrow definition of ethics, then the two directions justification can take are to be characterized as meta-ethical and pre-ethical. The meta-ethical justification moves upwards and logically or, through a decision, leaves ethics behind, whereas the pre-ethical justification moves downwards to the expressions of life.

Confrontation

In the final analysis, one's way of thinking about ethics depends on one's way of thinking about the relationship between humankind and the universe. This is also suggested by the discussion about naturalism—a discussion from which moral philosophy cannot easily detach itself.

During the biological development of humankind, humans were transformed over time from natural into cultural beings. What culture has brought with it is the distance to our surroundings and to those of our own actions in which knowledge and mastery, administration and planning, can unfold. Everyone can agree on this.

The paths diverge, however, when we consider the view of the universe on which the one and the other moral philosophy are based. My thesis is that when one does not go downwards to the expressions of life, it is because one assumes that the human as an ethical being does not belong to the universe. Humankind certainly issues from the universe, but as ethical beings we nonetheless have nothing to do with it.

This places moral philosophy in a predicament. Humankind brings the elemental needs from its natural history with it into its cultural history. What is added, however, is the difference between how a human being should and should not deal with these needs—both its own and those of other people. This difference is not to be found in the universe, or in the biological evolutionary process from which the needs arise. If humankind brings its cultural and ethical concerns to nature and to the universe, it will encounter only indifference.

Now the ethical precept's "ought" stands and falls with our being confronted with it. The question of where the precept's "ought" comes from is therefore unavoidable. Only two answers seem possible, and both seem to annul the "ought" of the precept. An "ought" that we ourselves create, we can also revoke, and then it is not an "ought," for we cannot be confronted with it. In order for us to be confronted with it, it would have had to come from the universe, but that, too, is out of the question. Our existence is of another nature than the existence of the universe. The upward-ascending path in moral philosophy leads to a dilemma we cannot escape.

But what then of the relationship between humankind and the universe if we take the path that leads downwards? As accounted for above, the norm's "ought" is a confrontation with the unconditionality of the expression of life, brought on by crisis and conflict. For this reason we are cut off from taking back the ethical "ought." We can disregard it, and largely do, but that is another matter.

Consider this example: Speech does not get its openness from the individual, nor from society, but from speech itself. But surely, speech gets its openness from our sincerity? No, quite the opposite. The individual sincerity is based on an openness in speech as a pre-individual expression of life. This appears from the fact that no matter how insincere we are, the openness of speech makes itself felt as a demand we disregard, and which we are most often aware of disregarding. Not only do we, by virtue of our topics and intentions, have some purpose with speech, but speech also has some purpose with us, by virtue of the openness that it simultaneously gives and demands. Perhaps the pre-individual quality of speech becomes clearer still when we contemplate the fact that we can only be insincere by means of the openness of speech. We can only be untruthful by dissimulation and by deceiving the other person. By what means? By the openness of speech. By this means we get the other to swallow the bait of our lies. We can only disregard the openness of speech by making it a feigned openness. Openness can never be eliminated, not even in the deepest deception. Mere speech involves it. It is just as much of a condition for lying as for telling the truth.

The expression of life is realized in the world of space and time. At the same time it is unconditional. It is both: empirical and unconditional. It is ours, but it is not we who create it. We cannot give an adequate portrayal of the way in which the expression of life makes itself felt and of the role it plays in the life of the individual, without assuming that its origins do not lie in the will and the resolution of the individual. We say: the expression of life has something to achieve, and to do this it must be latent. We cannot portray the expression of life without portraying it in its sovereignty in relation to the individual that identifies himself or herself with the expression. This indicates that the expression arises out of the nature and the universe in which the individual is embedded.

As mentioned earlier, if we leave the expression of life in the lurch, we are confronted with its unconditionality. Therefore its unconditionality bears witness to the fact that it is not created by us, but comes from the universe. A precondition for this, however, is that the being of the universe is not of a different nature than human existence as far as those aspects are concerned that are decisive for human beings.

This is undeniably at odds with the view of the universe we otherwise embrace. This is where the paths diverge. If we maintain that when bringing forward that which is important to us, we meet only indifference in the universe, then there is no room for the expressions of life and their unconditionality. They are eliminated. There is room only for needs.

This is characteristic of the situation of our civilization. Everything is a need. Anything that motivates and drives our existence is a need. The word "need" has gradually come to hold such an extensive meaning that it is virtually meaningless. But expressions of life are not needs. Mercy has to do with the needs of the person in distress, but not with the needs of the person showing mercy.

Expressions of life and norms must be kept separate from needs and evaluations. There is nothing ethical about deeming happiness to be a good thing and pain a bad thing. It is not ethical until one does one's part to free another person from pain and to give them a chance at happiness and flourishing. Mercy presupposes that happiness is sought after and pain is fought against, but that still does not make those two statements any more fundamental than mercy, since they are not yet ethical. They do not become ethical by being evaluations that are presuppositions of mercy. Pronouncements such as "happiness is good" and "pain is bad" are evaluations. They are analytical, as happiness has an inherently positive value, pain an inherently negative one. Their role in ethics is the result of their being presuppositions of an unconditional expression of life such as mercy, and therefore also presuppositions of the norms to which mercy gives rise. But precisely for this reason they themselves are not norms.

If we ask why we only take account of needs, the answer is straightforward: The human brings needs from its existence as a natural being with it into its existence as a cultural being. Needs do not render the relationship between the human being and the universe problematic, as the expressions of life do. The expressions of life prompt us to revise our view of the universe (a problem I will discuss in another publication, *Metafysik III*).

The expressions of life suggest a religious interpretation. I have dealt with this in *Skabelse og tilintegørelse* (Creation and Annihilation). When something as unconditional as an expression of life comes from the universe, the thought springs to mind that humankind is not irrelevant to the universe.

Notes

1. Translators' note: Here the Danish text uses *medlidenhed* rather than *barmhjertighed*, which is normally translated as "mercy."

2. Translators' note: This sentence is problematic, because the unconditional nature of the sovereign expressions of life for Løgstrup precisely implies that, in relevant cases, their *opposites* have to be justified (see, for example, his reflections on "suspending the expression of life" later in this extract). Therefore this sentence cannot be an objection to the claim that the sovereign expressions of life defy justification. Interestingly, an earlier version of this text (in translation) reads as follows: "Someone may say: But why is distrust not preferable to trust, hate to love, lies to truth?" (posthumous paper V.11.16.1, 7). This version is unproblematic, because it can be read as a challenge to justify the sovereign expressions of life. Cf. Kees van Kooten Niekerk, "Løgstrup on the Justification of the Sovereign Expressions of Life—a Textual Problem," in *Newsletter*, edited by the Løgstrup Archive, Summer 2004 (www.loegstrup.au.dk).

3. Translators' note: The Danish *afledbare*—"derivable"—in the original must be an error.

FIVE

Politics and Ethics

There are two different types of power. One is the immediate or strictly personal power that one person exercises over another. This is occasionally also referred to as psychological power. The underlying idea is that the life of one person is interwoven with that of another, that all relationships between people are, in the immediate sense, relationships of power. Another type of power is the power that has been delegated to a person. This power is public, often defined by laws governing how it should be exercised. This is sometimes referred to as power by virtue of authority. It serves to regulate our communal lives and to protect one person from violations perpetrated by another. This transports us into political life, the word "political" being applied very broadly. Here, however, we run into the view that ethics has very little to do with politics, and the commandment to love one's neighbor has nothing whatsoever to do with it. From many different sides—from among the ranks of social scientists and the ranks of theologians—attempts are being made to disengage ethics and politics. The social science justification is twofold: (a) economic life has become far too complicated to allow political decisions to be made on the basis of ideological and ethical viewpoints, and (b) ideology and ethics in politics serve no other purpose than to camouflage selfish interests. Or it is put this way: People's selfish interests express themselves in the economic laws. Not respecting them will lead to catastrophe. The Soviet Union's agricultural policy during Stalin's rule is a textbook example. Or references are made to wage policy, asserting that if everyone receives equal income, people will not work just as much as everyone else, but just as little, causing the total amount of work performed to decline, which will disadvantage everyone. Equal income for all will, in the long term, give everyone a lower standard of living—not just those whose pay is reduced, but also those whose pay initially increases.

Moving on to the theological justification for keeping ethics and politics clearly segregated, it also is twofold: (a) politics is about the collective order, while ethics in a radical sense belongs to individual interpersonal relations, and (b) ethics renders politics overly idealistic. So the question is: Can we effectively use ethical viewpoints in political life without becoming prone to excessive idealism and transferring that which only applies to individual interpersonal relations to the collective order?

What we will have to do is to moderate morality for use in our society; we must de-radicalize and de-emotionalize it. But then, one might immediately ask, why not just stick to a moderate morality that can readily be used politically, instead of going to a radical morality that must first be moderated to become politically applicable? There are two reasons for opting in favor of the latter: (1) it is not possible to conceive of a more natural morality than the ethical demand, which springs from the fundamental fact that there is an element of power in all our mutual relations with one another, and (2) the most natural morality conceivable is the most radical morality conceivable.

The Golden Rule

The most natural of all moral rules is the one known as "the Golden Rule," which states that what you would have others do unto you, you should do unto them. This is a very radical rule, thanks to the element of imagination it contains, and indeed depends on entirely, for here there is no mention of reciprocation. On the contrary. It is not based on establishing that since the other person actually took care of me, I must return the favor and take care of him or her. It does not consist in doling out assistance. It does not say: to the extent that another person helped me to flourish, so must I help that person to flourish. On the contrary, the Golden Rule is radical. It says that even though the other has done nothing for me, I am still to do for that person the things he or she is in need of. Perhaps the other person has never been in a position that enabled him to do anything for me. He may always have drawn the shortest straw in life. In brief, the rule does not apply to our experience of how much or how little the other has done for us. It appeals, rather, to our imagination: The charitable acts I might have wished another would do for me, had I been in his position, those acts should I do for him.

Whereas the wording of the love commandment emphasizes how our selfishness demonstrates that the most natural commandment is the most radical, the Golden Rule emphasizes the imaginative aspect.[1] But just as it is impossible for us to engage our nature in conforming to the commandment of love, it is equally impossible to do so in conforming to the Golden Rule. Consequently, we cannot arrange society based on an expectation that people will wholeheartedly conform to this rule. It goes without saying that this would be overly idealistic. Yet that does not mean ethics has nothing to do with politics. But it does require us to moderate the commandment and the rule for use in our society. This is not achieved by making the Golden Rule into a rule about reciprocation. Reciprocation serves no one, politically or otherwise. For as I have mentioned already, those who need our help are quite often the very people who have not been able to give anything in return, and who may never be able to do so. No, the moderation must consist in arranging society in such a way that the powerful are compelled to wield their power as though they had received it in order to serve others. In principle, we do this in public life by having power be an authority delegated to individuals—power with which these individuals are entrusted, and which they are held accountable for exercising appropriately.

Neighborly love as realization and idea

When life among people is spoken of in the proclamation of Jesus it is always, or almost always, in terms of individual facing individual. Humankind, the people, are left out of the story. It is always about my relationship to my neighbor. In the parable of the Good Samaritan, Jesus speaks of the relationship of the priest, the Levite, and the Samaritan to the waylaid man.

As it turns out, though, very few individual relationships are not somehow objectively mediated and do not involve political problems. It would be quite convenient if the Samaritan possessed some medical knowledge and knew something about how to treat wounds. At any rate, the Samaritan's mercy, which resulted in his tending to the waylaid man, was objectively—meaning in this case medically—mediated. And we can continue to elaborate on the account, imagining the Samaritan had been told at the inn that in those parts solitary travelers were often waylaid and assaulted. The next time he came to the capital, the Samaritan therefore brought it to the attention of the authorities that bands of robbers were on the rampage, making the region unsafe, and when the authorities refused to listen to his appeal, he attempted to rally popular opinion to put an end to this nuisance. The merciful Good Samaritan became a Political Samaritan. There is the connection that his mercy inspired him to his politics. But there is undeniably a difference as well. There, on the lonely road, the Samaritan realized the love of his neighbor, whereas in the Samaritan's political activity the love of his neighbor only functioned as an idea. But does the latter hold any meaning whatsoever? Is the commandment not subject to such transformations on the way from Jesus' talk of realizing it to the political conception of neighborly love as an idea that it loses its identity in the process? Simply operating with the idea does not require any love, nor does it require any neighbor, any more than it entails any costs. So does anything at all remain? Yes, something does remain: the changing of roles.

In the role-changing that takes place in the realization of neighborly love there is, as mentioned, an element of imagination, for its realization does not consist in one person making their way into the situation of the other person and becoming like the other. This would not lead to any change of roles, keeping in mind that the second person did not enter into the situation of the first simply because the first entered into the situation of the second. They merely both ended up in the same situation. It is therefore through imagination that individuals can put themselves in the place of another, proceeding to do that which the other would appreciate them doing. Realizing neighborly love consists in the individual actually doing these things. The changing of roles is formulated in the Golden Rule: Everything you wish people would do towards you—implying "if you were in their place"—you are to do towards them. This implied "if you were in their place" is the element of imagination, whereas "you are to do towards them" is the realization. The role-changing embodied in the Golden Rule is illustrated with the parable presented in Matthew 25. What you wish people would do towards you (visit you, if you were in prison), you are to do towards them (that is, visit them). The realization does not consist in becoming the other, in going to prison. That does not serve the other, for then he cannot be visited. Nor does the imprisoned person become free by the free person going to prison. The only result is that they both end up in prison. This is not how a change of roles is brought about. No, role-changing consists in imagining what help one would appreciate if one were in the other person's situation (in prison), and realization consists in providing that help.

A precondition for moving love of one's neighbor from realization to idea is that realizing it involves an element of imagination, namely the changing of roles. That moves with it. On the other hand, the deeds to which the role-changing is supposed to give rise are different. In the realization of it they are actions that take place in the individual relationship, whereas in the idea they constitute an activity that targets the social order.

When the Political Samaritan is inspired by neighborly love as an idea in his attempts to gain influence on the social order, he does not realize any love of his neighbor. In his political work he may forget those who were waylaid, becoming preoccupied with what it takes to create stability within the social order.

Nor is society arranged in such a way that people get the opportunity and the freedom to love their neighbor. Neither the politician nor the people do so when love of one's neighbor is taken as an idea. So who loves this neighbor? The answer is: no one. But then we must once again ask: Does anything remain of the commandment? Yes, something does remain.

Allow me to illustrate this using a contemporary and a historical example. Changing the arrangement of society towards a more equal distribution of income forces people to distribute consumer goods among themselves as though the strong loved the weak—completely ignoring how the strong gnash their teeth when their incomes are curtailed in favor of increasing the incomes of the weak. If we politically use love of one's neighbor as an idea, no one loves their neighbor, although some are compelled to act as though they did. Perhaps the strong agree to the arrangement out of an understandable interest in their own well-being, reasoning as follows: "Only by evening out income distribution will we be able to avoid an explosion that will blow us all away." And if they put up a fight, no one cares in the slightest. For although it is true that one can only love one's neighbor voluntarily, one can very well be forced to live as though one did, and a reasonable policy should seek this end. To make use of the Golden Rule as a political idea is to use the arrangement of society to have people act as though they loved their neighbor, knowing full well that they do not.

Now for the historical example.[2] Around 1700 there was a struggle in Denmark to obtain sufficient support for the poor to provide them with food and lodgings. There was also a wish to rid society of the ever-present beggars. The Danish government appointed commissions to come up with ways to procure the necessary capital, and to table proposals for making the collections door-to-door and in the churches more efficient. Certain visionary members of the commissions realized that the only viable way forward was to introduce a poverty tax, and that is what they proposed. Others refused to support the idea. Charity had to be voluntary, and compelling people to charity through taxation was both immoral and unchristian. Mandatory generosity would not allow a person to enter heaven. Following a compromise proposal that was still inadequate, Denmark ended up with the poverty ordinance of 1708. The ordinance was a step forward, although it, too, eventually proved insufficient.

This discussion shows that politically it does not do to accept that if the necessary attitude is lacking, the deeds will not be performed. What applies in politics is, however, that if the attitude is lacking, the deeds must be forced into existence.

It is important to establish that none of us loves our neighbor when we are politically inspired by the Golden Rule as an idea. Otherwise we entangle ourselves in a kind of hypocrisy that unavoidably gives rise to cynicism. Jørgen Jørgensen points out that in the love of ideas, not only is the idea assessed positively—that goes without saying—but so too is one's love of the idea. Not only the object (the idea) is held in high esteem, but so too is one's sentiment (one's love of the idea). One therefore has a tendency to make it look as though—in order to win the esteem of others and to ensure one's own self-esteem—one really feels love for the idea. This in turn means the goal is no longer to realize the idea, but to be regarded, in one's own eyes and the eyes of others, as one who has a love of the idea (*Psykologi på biologisk grundlag* [Psychology on a Biological Basis] [Copenhagen, 1941], 517). The two shifts to which Jørgen Jørgensen draws attention become all the more fatal when the idea in question is neighborly love. For this leads them to cause a third shift: the love of the idea is taken to be the love of one's neighbor. When one then seeks to make it appear as though one wishes to realize the idea out of neighborly love, the level of hypocrisy reaches enormous heights.

But to sum up: it corresponds to the element of *imagination* present in the role-changing that we, in politically using the Golden Rule as an idea, employing the force that is involved in the arrangement of society, have people *act as though* they lived by the Golden Rule.

Theodor Geiger's cardinal idea in *Die Gesellschaft zwischen Pathos und Nüchternheit* (Society between Pathos and Sobriety), from 1960, was that community of emotions, love, and sympathy belongs within small groups, not large ones. His claim is analogous to, if not identical with, the theological statement that loving one's neighbor is an individual relationship. On the other hand, the arrangements by which we manage our lives together in large groups become so technical and so comprehensive that it exceeds the individual's emotional scope to have a sympathetic relationship to the others with whom he or she has dealings or is dependent upon in this setting. The cooperation in the external interdependence can no longer be ensured spontaneously through the emotional community of the inner interdependence, and it must therefore be ensured by means of a purely objective order. Without mutual sympathy, people must learn to work together. Geiger is right on that point. But he is not right in the conclusion he reached, namely, that ideas must be eliminated from political life, and ethics along with them.[3] The thing Geiger failed to understand was that we can very well have the objective order of things be ethically inspired without claiming to realize emotional community. Politically we can and must arrange society as though we felt sympathy for one another, knowing full well that we do not.

And that is not all. We can by no means avoid arranging ourselves— either as though we wished to be considerate of one another or as though we only wished to do away with one another. Geiger was clinging to an illusion when he claimed that the political order could be purely objective. That is impossible; it is always ethical as well.

Notes

1. Translators' note: The comparison between the Golden Rule and the love commandment refers to an earlier passage of the present article, which is not included here. In that passage Løgstrup had interpreted the love commandment as "From the love you claim for yourself you know the love you owe to the other," thus connecting its naturalness and radicality with our selfishness.

2. Birgit Løgstrup, *Fattigvæsenet I København omkring 1700 med særlig henblik på fattigforordningen af 24.9.1708* (Poor Relief in Copenhagen around 1700 with Special Emphasis on the Poor Relief Ordinance of 24 September 1708) (history thesis, University of Copenhagen, 1967).

3. This conclusion also has other premises, but I have disregarded them here. I have considered them in my essay "Politisk ledelse og massehensyn" (Political Leadership and Regard for the Masses) in *Kunst og etik* (Art and Ethics), 1966.

SIX

Expressions of Life and Ideas

The expressions of life and the social order

If it is the spontaneous and sovereign expressions of life that engender ethics, any attempt to elucidate the relation between ethics and politics prompts the important question of how expressions of life relate to the social order. At first glance, they would seem to be mutually antithetical. The society in which we live is pervasively rationalized and organized. The expressions of life, by contrast, are not susceptible of rationalization and own no organizing power. This does not mean, however, that they are of no political significance, but it does mean—to anticipate the reflections that follow—that their role is something other and more important than that of rationalizing and organizing society.

The expressions of life and rationalization

In every quarter of the globe and throughout human history rationalization has been a reality, but nowhere on the scale seen in Western culture.

Above all else, rationality is the hallmark of modern society. Sociologically speaking, society comprises relatively autonomous sectors such as the judicial system, the economy, public administration, the sciences. So pervasively rationalized are the various domains that the lives of citizens, which are perforce played out within them, become computable; both in what concerns their own behavior and the experiences that they are likely to meet. Each of the institutional systems, which might also be called domains, effects this in its own peculiar way. Rationality is not a question of people being wiser now than they were in earlier times, but in our existence having become maximally computable.

The relative autonomy of the various domains does not mean that they are insulated from one another. Not only are they interconnected—they overlap. Rationalization also means that the domains are integrated into a comprehensive social structure, in which everything interacts with everything else. To offer just one example: with the emergence of research as an important source of wealth, there is no avoiding its integration in politics and administration, as so-called research policy shows.

Rationality is not a bad thing; we all benefit from it in manifold ways. We benefit from the rule of law. In virtue of the consumer goods with which we are supplied on a daily basis, we are the beneficiaries of rationalized production. Should we fall ill, we benefit from the medical sciences and an institutionalized health care system, and so I could continue.

But there are no advantages without drawbacks. There is undeniably a danger inherent in the pervasive rationalization of modern society, which consists, first and foremost, in its depersonalizing effects. Before we are aware of it, rationalization is being pursued for its own sake and becomes increasingly abstract. There is a weakening of the sense of the independence and sui generis nature of the expressions of life that sustain rationality without being themselves susceptible of rationalization. Their content is diluted and they become etiolated, and the awareness of how crucially they sustain a social life of substance and vibrancy is lost. To counter impersonalization, to keep it at bay so that it does not get the upper hand, we need to reflect on and distinguish between what can be rationalized and what cannot.

The need for food, warmth, a roof over one's head, is amenable to rationalization, and is indeed rationalized in the industrial production of goods that supply these needs. And needs multiply. Basic needs may well remain the same but they undergo refinement, and proliferate as they do so. The need for food becomes subject to gastronomic refinements and variation so that it comes finally to encompass a whole cluster of needs. The need for a roof over one's head is refined aesthetically and allows for varied architectural expression, so that it too comprises an entire cluster of needs.

What, by contrast, are unrationalizable are our expressions of life—trust, openness, indignation, compassion, hope. They have persisted unchanged from the beginning of time to the present and are constants in our life. Once apprehended in thought, they cannot be unthought. They are not refinable, nor can they become more numerous. Should an expression of life be lost, no amount of rationalization can compensate for it. They are not irrational: they have a primordiality which precedes any distinction between rationality and irrationality. Taken together, the unrationalizable expressions of life form the foundation upon which our rational endeavors build. Without them, the whole of our pervasively rationalized social structure would collapse.

The expressions of life and organization

What can be the reason for our neglecting the expressions of life to the extent that we do? In the first place, it is due to the fact that they are latencies, or should be. But why do we go on neglecting them even after our dereliction has made us aware of them? That is a consequence of the fact that they are without the power to organize society; their unconditionality renders them incapable of that. However, so preoccupied are we with the organizing of our existence that phenomena not conducive to that end are ones we barely heed, even though all organization necessarily hinges around them if it is not to be futile or make everything worse.

For the organization of actions and initiatives, conditional as they always are, ideals are needed. We have to distinguish, then, between the expressions of life that create and sustain our lives—and, on the other hand, the ideas with which we organize life in society.

Those ideas are constantly revisable, which the expressions of life are not. The question is, then: What is the nature of the positive and the negative interaction between expressions of life and ideas? I shall cite two examples.

I take my first example from Richardt Hansen's dissertation, *Spontaneität, Geschichtlichkeit, Glaube* (Spontaneity, Historicity, Faith) (Regensburger Studien zur Theologie, vol. 10 [Frankfurt a. M., 1978], 42–43). We should be unable to acquaint ourselves with an existent body of theoretical knowledge, and incapable of sharing it with one another, were trust not part of our existence. But trust takes different forms. In our acceptance of theoretical knowledge, trust is not spontaneously and sovereignly present as it is in our social exchanges and our common life. It is present as an idea. This is also true with regard to the "community of scientists," which plays a very prominent role in the organization of the pursuit of science, especially in the exact sciences, and indeed in the theory of science too, as shown in Peter Skagestad's dissertation, *Making of History* ([Oslo, 1975], 26). The relation between expression of life and idea is in this case as follows: In and of itself trust owns no organizing power; it connects with organization only when it is translated into an idea or gives impetus to ideas. But ideas presuppose the expression of life. Without trust as a spontaneous and sovereign expression of life, no organized "community of scientists" could have emerged.

But the relation between expression of life and idea can take a different form and does so in my second example, which concerns the idea of equality. Compared with earlier periods, equality has played an extremely important role in recent times and continues to do so. The first thing to be said about equality is that it is not an attribute of persons, but that persons are situated as equals in this, that, or the other respect, and that despite their inequality. It is not in dispute whether individuals should be situated as equals with regard to educational opportunity. It *is* in dispute whether they are to be situated as equals economically.

There is, nowadays, a tendency to want to justify equal treatment by saying that people are equal in terms of their equipment, an equality sometimes also referred to as biological. Biologically, people are born equal, it is claimed, and if this biological equality is lost, the environment is the cause. This line of thinking is abstract and divorced from reality. Equality is a condition that comes about solely through one person making the other his equal, or through society rendering all equal before the law and at the ballot box, despite inequalities in equipment.

The leveling of incomes is a political task and consists in making people equal, so far as is feasible, in economic terms. But it is not the task

of the school to deliver a basis for this political aspiration by doing everything in its power to bring it about that young people leave school as equal
in equipment, physical and intellectual, as possible. It is a political task to
bring it about that, before the law and with regard to opportunities for the
exercise of political influence as well as economically, the young person
who becomes a sewage worker is placed on equal terms with the young
person who becomes a nuclear physicist, and it is not the school's object to
neutralize the biological differences between the two. The school is not
charged with the delivery of a biological basis for political equality.

The question then arises as to why, in our societies, we seek to make
people equal in this, that, or the other regard. The answer is that we do so
to secure their freedom and promote their independence. It belongs to
freedom and independence to develop one's abilities and skills in one's
own way, to the extent that circumstances permit. Through situating
people equally—and here I wish to stress that equality is a relation into
which we are placed—society seeks to secure human flourishing across
inequalities to the greatest possible extent. The idea is that equality of status will create individual space, scope, and opportunity. It is important
that we are situated as equals precisely because we are so unequal.

Above all else, equality has become an idea informing the organization of society. There are those who contend that not only is it the most
important, but it is the only one we have. It is a new idea; the question is
how and when it arose.

It was once assumed that the distribution of power and the social
order were fixed for all time and foreordained. This assumption held sway
throughout much the greater part of the history of humankind. Corre-
spondingly, the justification given for both the distribution of power and
the social order had therefore to be that these things were immutable and
preempted human beings. This state of affairs was something the justification was required to explain and it did, manifold though the forms taken
by the explanation might be. It was argued that the distribution of power
and the social order were contingent on human nature or on the nature of
society as such, or it was said that they were a reflection of the cosmic
order or that they were anchored in the will of God. But what all the justi-
fications had in common was that they were absolutist. The justification
was as absolute as the social order was firmly fixed and foreordained. To
organize society according to one's own ideas was out of the question;

human beings were to accept the social order as it had been determined by higher powers, beyond human reach, irrespective of whether these powers were constituted by their own nature, the cosmos, or God.

The epoch in which we live, and which we call the new or the modern era, is in part the result of the realization that neither the distribution of power nor the social order is fixed, nor are they foreordained, but they are ours to determine. For it is up to human beings themselves to distribute power, it is for them to organize themselves socially and politically. With the belief that the social order is ours to determine, the absolutist justification falls away—which gives the idea of equality its chance. If neither nature nor the cosmos nor God determines, once and for all, authority or the social order, why should not each individual person be party to its determination? Equality moves into the space vacated by the collapse of the absolutist idea, a collapse that followed in the wake of the realization that we are responsible for the social order. I am following here the account of the German sociologist of knowledge Günter Dux, which reads: Once an absolutist justification is abandoned, there remains just one justification for the ordering of the social world, and its name is equality. Only equality is capable of winning a consensus. Dux also sums up the transformation that takes place by saying that whereas, previously, the question was what rendered existing law binding, now the question is that of what the law must be like to be accounted binding. Now it is a matter of discovering which order is arguably legitimate (Günter Dux, *Strukturwandel der Legitimation* [Structural Change in Legitimation] [Freiburg i. Breisgau, 1976], 337).

But if it is correct that the organization of the social order has nothing other to base itself on than the idea of equality, we find ourselves in a severe predicament. For there are limits to what the idea of equality is well suited to organize, and if we attempt to overextend its use, it will prove itself an arid and harsh principle.

There is something the idea of equality is good for. No individual can exist without being subject to the exercise of power. Equality does not consist in living in a power vacuum, for none such exists. Equality consists in having a say in how the power to which one is oneself subject shall be configured.

But is equality not suited to the organization of justice? Is the principle that all are equal before the law not a supreme principle? No. One of the principal ideas behind law enforcement has indeed been a polemic against the idea of equality. The polemic is expressed in the dictum: strict justice is the greatest injustice. The meaning of the dictum is that the more consistently the assumption that society consists of entirely equal legal persons is acted upon, the greater the injustice that will result from law enforcement. For then the fundamental fact that individuals are unequal in all sorts of respects is ignored. Justice that does not proceed from, and fails to respect, the differences between persons becomes a mask for injustice.

The question is how far a judicious and fruitful use of the idea of equality extends, and at what point it turns into something unprofitable and harsh. It is a safeguard and a weapon against the arbitrary distribution of power and the arbitrary exercise of power. It is to this that its popularity is due. But if our use of it goes beyond that, if we use it to drive out inequality, then its function is to allow us with a good conscience to be unconcerned about those who fall by the wayside. If equality seeks to replace inequality—in the sphere of human aptitudes, in the sphere of equipment that is biologically conditioned—it becomes an unprofitable and harsh principle. If we say, for example: everyone must have the same opportunities—we use the equality principle as a safeguard and weapon against arbitrariness, against privilege. If we go further and say: now that everyone has been given the same opportunities, each person must make out as well as he or she can—we are acting as though people were equal in respect of their aptitudes and equipment. Equality has now supplanted inequality and has become a principle for the promotion of ruthless competition, an all-out struggle. The difficulty is that as effective as the idea of equality is in motivating revolt, it is equally unsuitable to organize every sphere of the society whose emergence the revolt was intended to mediate. The idea of organizing society by using the very idea that proved itself eminently suited to the conduct of revolt is a seductive and natural one; but the result is dismal for those who suffer the consequences of that equality, which is to say, the majority.

But whence do we learn when the idea of equality is indeed life-affirming and when it is life-denying? From the expressions of life! Mercy draws the line between what the idea of equality is well suited to organize and what it is not. It is not, as was once believed, the distribution of power that is unconditional: it is the expressions of life.

Using the expressions of life to test the idea

The upshot of the foregoing reflections is twofold: the expressions of life sustain all rationalization and organization. The ideas grounding our rationalizing and organizing must constantly be tested against the expressions of life.

This invites the following fallacy: Since the expressions of life are the foundation of the social order—since, in the final analysis, all politics reposes upon the expressions of life—our task must be to draw from the expressions of life the ideas for the organization of society. But this simply cannot be done, inasmuch as the expressions of life have no organizing power intrinsic to themselves. They have, as has been noted several times already, a more important role, which is that of sustaining the whole. Nor is it possible to ground the ideas by reference to the expressions of life. It does not follow from the fact that the ideas have to be tested against expressions of life that they can be grounded in them. That is not possible on account of the fact that they originate elsewhere. The idea of equality, as we have seen, arises from the collapse of the absolutist conception.

We are misguided if we seek to derive ideas from or justify them by reference to the expressions of life. To do so is to imagine that society could be founded on a high-minded morality. It is to dream of a social order to which we are not morally equal. We should content ourselves instead with asking whether our ideas banish the expressions of life from the social order. Let me illustrate my distinction between the organizing ideas and the sustaining expressions of life by testing it against Ole Thyssen's attack (in his essay "Den Anden Natur" [Second Nature] in the anthology *Spurvens Vilje* [The Will of the Sparrow]) on what he calls Christian morality. (My reluctance, without qualification, to call that morality Christian is based on a number of considerations which I shall not enter into here. I am also given pause by my wish to respect the fact that Ole Thyssen subscribes to its content, or at least as much of it as is relevant in the present context. If I have understood Ole Thyssen correctly, it is not, properly speaking, its content that he attacks, but the illusion of its usability).

In his rejection of Christian morality, Ole Thyssen offers a characterization of it that I am able to endorse but which I do not see as providing reasons for its rejection. In other words, as well judged as the attack may be, in equal measure, it seems to me, its target is misconceived.

Ole Thyssen levels two objections against Christian morality: its requirements are minimal and its requirements are radical. There is no contradiction between these two objections for the perspectives are distinct in each case. If we consider the usability of Christian morality for the solution of wholly specific social problems and for the overcoming of wholly specific difficulties, its requirements show themselves to be quite devoid of prescriptions. They are too minimal to be used to any political end. In Ole Thyssen's own words, they abstract away from all concrete relations between people and are therefore eminently adaptable to many different kinds of society. If we consider our chances of fulfilling the demands, these latter prove to be so radical that only exceptional individuals have any possibility of succeeding. In short, both in what concerns their minimalism and in what concerns their radicalism, the demands are unusable.

I shall now engage with Ole Thyssen's objections in order to assess them. He is correct in claiming that the requirements are minimal. But unlike him I find them no less usable and relevant for that. Not only are they violated, their moral status is positively denied. In his analysis of Nazism, Harald Ofstad has shown that its most signal feature was contempt for whatever is weak (*Vårt förakt för Svaghet: Nazismens Normer och Vurderinger och var Tid* [Our Contempt for Weakness: Nazism's Norms and Values and Our Times], 1972). Nazism not only abrogated the requirement that we care for the weak, it failed to recognize it as moral; indeed, it was considered immoral.

Ole Thyssen calls the demands minimal, but he might equally have called them trivial. If on this basis he were to call Christian morality trivial, I would also agree with him in that characterization. I would merely add that there is no reason to neglect the trivial, for it is ultimately the most important thing in our lives. Disasters result when we ignore it.

In what concerns Ole Thyssen's second objection, I also agree with him in thinking that the requirements are radical. But when he goes on to say that the radicalism of Christian morality blinds it to the complexities of everyday life, rendering that morality impotent once power asserts itself and power and property have to be distributed, he overlooks the distinction that is crucial here. The expressions of life—mercy, above all—in which the requirements are grounded have in themselves no power to order society. If one appraises Christian morality, as Ole Thyssen does, on the basis of its capacity to organize, it is indeed otiose. But I am unable to recognize the appropriateness of assessing Christian morality in terms of a power which, given its constitution, it lacks.

But if the expressions of life articulated in Christian morality do not organize society, what do they do? The answer is: they sustain the whole. They form the indispensable underpinning. It is the significance of that which needs to be engaged with when we are considering what Ole Thyssen calls Christian morality.

This is not to say that there is no connection between Christian morality and the political order and its distribution of power. Since the expressions of life sustain all fellowship and life in the community, it follows that they are the touchstone of fellowship and life in the community. But to repeat: they function as a criterion, not as the purveyors of prescriptions for social organization. Christianity does not organize society for us; that we must do ourselves. But not without criteria.

Were Ole Thyssen to redirect his attack, I would have no objections. Instead of directing his attack towards Christian morality, he should redirect it against two other targets: against the illusions entertained by Christians about what Christian morality is capable of organizing, and against the failure of Christians to test the social order against the expressions of life that are its underpinning.

Using problems to test the ideas

Liberal economics is testable by reference to the expressions of life. I have so tested it by asking whether a free pricing policy means that war, in the sense of intensified competition, is built into liberal economics and its social order. In a later essay I will test Marx's philosophy by reference to the expressions of life.[1]

Whence come the ideas with which we organize life in society? What suggests them to us? Certainly, the difficulties we have run into do. In the foregoing, then, and in no small measure, I have tested liberal economics by asking whether it is capable of overcoming our present difficulties. For they are new difficulties, and their novelty resides in the fact that they come from the same source as our welfare. The drawbacks have the same provenance as the advantages. Both stem from technology. While welfare and benefits derive from the goals that structure the technological enterprise, the difficulties and drawbacks are produced by the side effects to which that technological enterprise gives rise. The ideas for the organization of society that we are after are, therefore, ideas that enable us to retain those benefits of technology that have no threatening side effects—neither in the long term nor in the short term. The ideas that the liberal economist offers, and for which he is anxious to claim a place in a mixed economy, are free price-setting and the idea that production ought to be influenced only by indirect means.

We have two questions, then, to put to systems of ideas such as liberal economics and Marx's philosophy: Do they accommodate the expressions of life that sustain the whole? Are their ideas, elicited by dangers, capable of averting those dangers? Thorlund Jepsen responded to both questions in the affirmative: free price-setting is not necessarily bound up with marketplace wars in the form of cutthroat competition. Influencing production by indirect means is the best way of surmounting the difficulties we face. I begged leave to have my doubts.

The relation between political and cosmic equality

One question remains. Is there not, behind or beneath all inequalities, a deeper, underlying equality which grounds political equality? Is there not an equality into which we are placed not, first, politically, but in which, by the hand of nature, we already find ourselves? There is indeed. But it would seem only to be susceptible of negative formulation. But to the extent that it is formulable, what it says is clear: Letting a person's importance depend on his contribution to the common good is inhumanity. So doing would make cruelty towards the impecunious and the disadvantaged a guiding principle in our organization of society. If we include in the measure of a person's worth his contribution to the common good, there is no such thing as human rights.

Concerning much that obtains and occurs we can pose the question: In which respects is it to the good, and in which respects does it engender harm? We cannot pose that question about a human being; yes, in respect of a person's behavior and conduct, acts and deeds, but not in respect of his or her existence. The individual who from birth has been incapacitated by illness and has been unable to accomplish anything is above that question.

Concerning everything that obtains and occurs we can pose two questions: Has it a purpose and, if so, which? Or is it purposeless? Neither of those questions are ones we can pose in respect of any person's existence. A human existence is above being made the means to any end, and it is above being regarded as purposeless. Purposive or purposeless, that either-or gets no purchase on a person's life. In short, there exists no measure for a person's significance or worth, and in the absence of a measure, people are equal. That species of equality, too, we must give a name, and I propose that we call it cosmic. I shall explain why in a moment.

Two things follow from this. First, what democratic equalities are to consist in, how they are to be formulated, and how they are to function, is not something we can deduce from cosmic equality. For then we would be forgetting the inequalities of expertise and education, something that we cannot do since we use them in organizing society. Were we to deduce democratic equalities from cosmic equality we would also be disregarding the fact that the forms assumed by political equality are determined by the way history unfolds and by the era in which we live. Democratic equalities are forever being transformed. Marx's insight to the effect that they are determined by the conditions of production is beyond dispute. That insight has become the received wisdom. Today, we are led to invest democratic equalities with the forms and functions that enable them to avert the dangers threatened by the rule of experts.

This does not mean, however, that there is no relation between cosmic equality and political equality. Cosmic equality is the precondition of all democratic equality. The important point is that the relation is not a derivation. In a sense, the relation is more intimate than that, for it consists in the fact that cosmic equality sustains the whole—all fellowship and all life in the community. Our social order must constantly be held to account at the bar of cosmic equality: it is a touchstone, a criterion for our social order, but admits of no deduction.

This brings me to the second point that follows from cosmic equality, to the effect that the political order is judged according to the consideration it shows the weak, the impecunious, and the disadvantaged in society. This point is always relevant, for we are continually in the business of assessing an individual's behavior and conduct, acts and deeds, according to what he contributes to the common good.

But why do I call it cosmic? We can either consider the universe from the perspective of human existence, or we can consider human existence from the perspective of the universe. If we consider the universe from the perspective of human existence it reduces to the surroundings for our existence, in which case the fact that human existence forbids every mode of measurement calls for no explanation.

But if we consider human existence from the point of view of the universe, what requires an explanation is how, from the biological evolution on our planet, which is estimated to have spanned one to two billion years, it was possible for an existence such as that of human beings to emerge, one prohibiting the application of any measure.

What is most important—that the universe is what surrounds us, or that it is the source of our existence? There is no doubt as to the answer. What is most important is the fact that the universe is the source of our existence. Even today, it is this circumstance that effects our integration with the universe through our senses and, through our respiration and metabolism, with the ecology of nature. Again, as with everything else, we owe to the universe the equality that consists in no individual's existence being judged according to what he contributes to the common good, and for that reason I call this equality cosmic.

Another reason for calling this equality cosmic is that its cosmic nature explains why we cannot derive political equalities from it. The cosmos cannot organize our society for us; that we must do ourselves. It is we who must hit upon the ideas and set in place the arrangements that are needed to overcome the difficulties we encounter. Those arrangements include the democratic equalities. But our ideas and arrangements are constantly called before the bar of cosmic equality, which is, note, a tribunal, not an administrator or organizer.

We resist the idea that we owe equality to the universe. That is another reason for calling it cosmic. Our resistance to the notion that equality originated from the universe derives from our inability to account for it.

For it is inexplicable how an existence, conditioned and transitory, conditional upon evolution, which in turn is conditional upon constellations out in infinite space, stands or falls with its unconditionality.

We are dealing here, then, with three entities: cosmic equality, the inequalities of expertise and education, and the political or democratic equalities. Two questions present themselves. What is the relation between political equalities and, on the one hand, the inequalities of expertise and education, and on the other, cosmic equality? These questions give rise to two theses. The one runs: Inequalities and political equalities constitute a unifying opposition. The other runs: The political equalities are not derivable from cosmic equality inasmuch as cosmic equality is engaged in something more important, namely, the sustaining of the whole.

I want now to return to political equality and examine its relation to the structures of authority.

From reverence, to prestige, to expertise

A glance back over human history suggests that societies have never been able to function without structures of authority. This becomes especially clear at the very point at which the idea of equality won general acceptance—in the eighteenth century, with its declarations of human rights. It was not unusual at that time to think that people could not be situated as equals unless a monarch invested with absolute power decreed it. This should not be understood to mean that the absolutist monarch was temporarily, instrumentally necessary to divest the aristocratic regime of the power with which the patrimonial constitution had invested it. Rather, his authority alone was capable of guaranteeing equality. The absolute ruler was not merely needed to establish equality for a transition period, but was at all times needed to maintain it.

The structures of authority have their own history and are colored by the changing patterns of societal organization. There was a time when the structure of authority was a structure of reverence—that was when the constitution was patrimonial. It was Max Weber who characterized the authority of that time as reverential. When liberalism gains the ascendancy, the structure of authority becomes a structure of prestige. This was reflected in the rise of portraiture, which enjoyed a heyday. This is not to suggest that portraiture only served prestige. There were painters of too great a stature to go along with that. In their portraits, it is the person situated in his own solitudinous life who, in disregard of all prestige and in the absence of any onlookers, fixes his gaze upon the viewer, as does, for instance, the ageing Georg Brandes in Max Liebermann's brilliant portrait of him. What conferred prestige varied greatly. The European scientist who went to America after the Second World War to learn of the advances made in his field during the war could speak of the superior conditions for research in America. But no one wanted to swap places, since in America it was money that conferred prestige, whereas in Europe science did.

Today prestige is on the way out. Two tendencies in mutual contention occupy the scene. One is the rule of experts; the other is the idea of emancipation—the belief that society and its institutions can manage without structures of authority. That conflict has been assessed in the foregoing. Here it remains merely to add that the more the structures of authority crumble or are swept away, the more important becomes the sense of those sovereignties on which our existence reposes. If the sovereignties fail to fill the gap left by the structures of authority, the result will be social disintegration. But if we allow the sovereignties due scope, the loss of the structures of authority has its advantages. These latter have very often been arbitrary and, in the case of rule by experts, the threat of asinine interventions looms.

The sovereignties in our lives, which include perception and language, are anonymous in character and yet are ours. They are ours to the extent that we are capable of destroying them. They are anonymous to the extent that we cannot destroy them without destroying ourselves. We are in their power, but they do not intimidate us. We are identical with them, and they are liberating.

An exception: The parliamentary assembly

One of the biggest problems facing us today is how to mount an attack against the structures of authority without the structures of trust being forfeited in the process. This makes it all the more remarkable that there is one place in our society that is entirely unaffected by that problem.

Compared with other institutions, not to mention private companies, parliament, regional councils, and local councils have the huge advantage that they are without structures of authority. There is no assembly charged with specific tasks that is so utterly without structures of authority as is the parliamentary assembly. It is a precondition of the struggle for power being so relentless there, with that relentlessness constitutive of its health. No flouting of authority, no revolt, no insubordination is involved in the struggle for power. What a privilege it is indeed to be a politician! All are on an equal footing. Yes, in principle, but not in reality, it will be objected. What about the bruisers? What about the tables in the refreshment room! Who sits where? Granted, that is a valid point. But the principle is far from negligible. It means at least one thing: it means that what is required of a politician if he or she is to enter the fray is fearlessness, and fearlessness is a political quality of the first order. Objectivity matched by fearlessness hallmarks the individual who is a politician by nature. There is one place in our society, and perhaps uniquely one, where equality qua political principle presents no problem.

I said that the relentlessness of the struggle for power constitutes its health. This is manifest in the fact that there is one thing there is no room for in parliament, and—to limit myself to just one thing—that is the taking of offence. The individual who seeks to have his will prevail by threatening to take it very amiss if he is baulked is finished as a politician on the spot. He is steered out of the door without further ado. If one considers the extent to which the taking of offence wreaks havoc in our lives, how many human relationships founder upon it, it is quite extraordinary that there should exist an assembly where the taking of offence is not tolerated. But it would also appear that the only thing capable of banishing it is a relentless struggle for power.

In all other contexts, the relation between trust and the structures of authority is a vexed one. When a person has the necessary competence to solve certain tasks, and when the education he has received and the equipment that is concomitant upon it confers authority on him, resentment lies in wait. He is offended if his authority is not duly respected, and the others are offended if he uses his authority to slight them. They are on the lookout for the least abuse of authority; revolt lurks in the offing. Our society has become a society of individuals imbued with a sense of personal affront. Let us not pull the wool over our eyes: equality is the cause.

Equality has led to one sense being sharpened to the utmost—the sense of not receiving one's due. Politicians aside, there is no group in society that does not feel itself victimized. This is the situation into which equality has plunged us. But we cannot solve the problem as politicians do, because the parliamentary assembly is an exception and there is none like it.

That same parliamentary assembly places a ubiquitous phenomenon in a singular and revealing light. In the parliamentary assembly, negotiation is necessary. Under the guise of negotiation a battle must be waged. This is impossible without ground rules, and such rules are founded in the structures of trust. Or, more accurately, ground rules constitute the structure that trust assumes when it seeks a result via negotiation. If the ground rules are ignored, it spells the end of everything. That was what happened in the Weimar Republic. Between them, the two extremist blocs—the Nazis and the Communists—stifled everything else, and the day dawned that saw them resorting to violence and hurling inkwells at each other. Then it becomes manifest how irreplaceable the ground rules are. Once they are forfeited, no standing orders will make up for them, irrespective of how well thought-out or admirable these might be. This is by reason of the fact that in standing orders there is not the spontaneity that there is in ground rules, and the spontaneous expressions of life are what ultimately sustain the whole. Even so extreme a phenomenon as the relentless struggle for power resides in something as spontaneous as a structure of trust.

Notes

1. Translators' note: Løgstrup's essays on testing liberal economics and Marx's philosophy are not contained in this volume. The motivation for the inclusion of this paragraph is that it introduces those that follow.

Index

absolute, the, 67, 74
absurdity, 21
action, 130–32
adult, 3
Åhgren, Ulla, 31–32
Almond, Brenda, xxxi n7
altruism, 32
analysis, phenomenological, 7–8, 10, 11,
  13, 20, 41. *See also* phenomenology
appeal, 117–18
a priori, 39–40
Arendt, Rudolf, 39–45
argumentation, ethical, 103–5, 108–9,
  111, 118–19
Aristotle, 23
attitude, 98–99
  of mind, 63, 77, 85
Augustine, 14
authenticity, xvii
authority
  —absolute, 11

—structure(s) of, 162–64
  · —ultimate, xxi, xxiv, 33, 134

badness, 114–18
Barth, Karl, xxx n2, 20–21
belief, Christian, xiv, xvii, 32. *See also*
  faith, Christian
Blegvad, Mogens, 96, 101–2
Bloemhof, Dr., 26
Brandes, Georg, 163
British moral philosophy, 96–102,
  113–14, 117
Broch, Hermann, 65
Bukdahl, Jørgen K., 79, 82n5

Camus, Albert, 21
care, taking, 8, 10
certainty, 16–17
character, 92, 95, 123–25, 127–28
character trait(s), xix, xxi–xxii, 88–89,
  91–93, 124–25

K. E. Logstrup (1905–1981)

was professor of ethics and philosophy of religion at the University of
Aarhus until his retirement in 1975. He is the author of *The Ethical
Demand* (University of Notre Dame Press, 1997) and numerous books
and essays in Danish.